What Is Marriage?

What Is Marriage?

Man and Woman: A Defense

Sherif Girgis, Ryan T. Anderson,
and Robert P. George

ENCOUNTER BOOKS
New York · London

First American edition published in 2012 by Encounter Books,
an activity of Encounter for Culture and Education, Inc.,
a nonprofit, tax exempt corporation.
Encounter Books website address: www.encounterbooks.com

Manufactured in the United States and printed on
acid-free paper. The paper used in this publication meets
the minimum requirements of ANSI/NISO Z39.48–1992
(R 1997) (*Permanence of Paper*).

First paperback edition published in 2012.
Original paperback edition ISBN: 978-1-59403-622-4
Second paperback edition published in 2020.
Second paperback edition ISBN: 987-1-64177-147-4

THE LIBRARY OF CONGRESS HAS CATALOGUED
THE ORIGINAL PAPERBACK EDITION AS FOLLOWS:
Girgis, Sherif, 1986-
What is marriage? : man and woman : a defense /
by Sherif Girgis, Ryan T. Anderson, and Robert P. George.
p. cm.
Includes bibliographical references and index.
ISBN 978-1-59403-622-4 (hbk. : alk. paper) — ISBN 978-1-59403-623-1 (ebook)
1. Civil marriage   2. Marriage law.   3. Marriage.
I. George, Robert P.   II. Anderson, Ryan T., 1981–   III. Title.
HQ1001.G57 2012
306.81—dc23
2012007621

The extract from the poem "Epithalamion," by Sir Edmund Spenser,
has been reproduced from *The Oxford Book of English Verse, 1250–1900*,
edited by A. T. Quiller-Couch (Oxford: Clarendon Press, 1900).

PRODUCED BY WILSTED & TAYLOR PUBLISHING SERVICES
*Designer and composito*r Yvonne Tsang
Proofreader Melody Lacina

For our parents

Contents

A Note on Authorship

This book has been a collaborative project. Sherif Girgis is listed as first author to reflect his primary role in developing our arguments, and in drafting this book and the article on which it expands. Variations of some of the arguments of chapter 2 have been developed over several years by Germain Grisez, John Finnis, Joseph M. Boyle, Jr., Robert P. George, Patrick Lee, Christopher Tollefsen, Gerard Bradley, and Alex Pruss, among others. This book contains refinements in that chapter, and new arguments on related issues in every chapter, made by Girgis as well as by Ryan T. Anderson, who took the lead in shaping the book's structure.

Acknowledgments

This essay was born as an article before it matured into a book, and it has benefited from extensive help at every stage of its development. Special thanks go to Stefan McDaniel and John Finnis for close readings of the article and book drafts. For valuable comments on one or the other, we also thank Ron Belgau, Maggie Gallagher, Germain Grisez, Patrick Lee, Colin Moran, David Oakley, Matthew O'Brien, Nathaniel Peters, Alex Pruss, Nathaniel Schlueter, and Christopher Tollefsen. Their willingness to help was no endorsement of our claims, and we alone bear responsibility for any errors.

We thank the *Harvard Journal of Law and Public Policy* for editing and publishing "What Is Marriage?" and for giving us permission to publish this much-expanded version of it. Some material has also been taken from replies to critics that we published in the online journal *Public Discourse*. Finally, we are grateful to Roger Kimball, Heather Ohle, and the staff of Encounter Books for their confidence in this project's promise, and patience with its progress.

from Epithalamion

Edmund Spenser

And thou, great Juno! which with awful might
The lawes of wedlock still dost patronize;
And the religion of the faith first plight
With sacred rites hast taught to solemnize;
And eeke for comfort often callèd art
Of women in their smart;
Eternally bind thou this lovely band,
And all thy blessings unto us impart.
And thou, glad Genius! in whose gentle hand
The bridale bowre and geniall bed remaine,
Without blemish or staine;
And the sweet pleasures of theyr loves delight
With secret ayde doest succour and supply,
Till they bring forth the fruitfull progeny;
Send us the timely fruit of this same night.
And thou, fayre Hebe! and thou, Hymen free!
Grant that it may so be.

Til which we cease your further prayse to sing;
Ne any woods shall answer, nor your Eccho ring.

And ye high heavens, the temple of the gods,
In which a thousand torches flaming bright
Doe burne, that to us wretched earthly clods
In dreadful darknesse lend desirèd light;
And all ye powers which in the same remayne,
More then we men can fayne!
Poure out your blessing on us plentiously,
And happy influence upon us raine,
That we may raise a large posterity,
Which from the earth, which they may long possesse
With lasting happinesse,
Up to your haughty pallaces may mount;
And, for the guerdon of theyr glorious merit,
May heavenly tabernacles there inherit,
Of blessèd Saints for to increase the count.
So let us rest, sweet love, in hope of this,
And cease till then our tymely joyes to sing:
The woods no more us answer, nor our eccho ring!

Song! made in lieu of many ornaments,
With which my love should duly have been dect,
Which cutting off through hasty accidents,
Ye would not stay your dew time to expect,
But promist both to recompens;
Be unto her a goodly ornament,
And for short time an endlesse moniment.

What Is Marriage?

Introduction

TWO VIEWS OF MARRIAGE

What we have come to call the gay marriage debate is not directly about homosexuality, but about marriage. It is not about whom to let marry, but about what marriage is. It is a pivotal stage in a decades-long struggle between two views of the meaning of marriage.

The *conjugal* view of marriage has long informed the law—along with the literature, art, philosophy, religion, and social practice—of our civilization (see chapter 3). It is a vision of marriage as a bodily as well as an emotional and spiritual bond, distinguished thus by its comprehensiveness, which is, like all love, *effusive*: flowing out into the wide sharing of family life and ahead to lifelong fidelity. In marriage, so understood, the world rests its hope and finds ultimate renewal.

A second, *revisionist* view has informed the marriage policy reforms of the last several decades. It is a vision of marriage as, in essence, a loving emotional bond, one distinguished by its intensity—a bond that needn't point beyond the partners, in which fidelity is ultimately subject to one's own desires. In marriage, so understood, partners seek emotional fulfillment, and remain as long as they find it.

ɔ   ɔ   ɔ

In 1595, Edmund Spenser published an ode to Elizabeth Brody on the occasion of their wedding. "Epithalamion," meant as an "an endless monument" to the bride, also gives lasting poetic effect to the beauty, audacity, and reach of the first view of marriage mentioned above.

At the center of Spenser's poem—and thus central to marriage —is the spouses' union of body and mind. The bridegroom-speaker devotes four central stanzas to his bride's "body like a palace fair," then to her "inward beauty," to their spiritual union by vows, and then to their bodily union by consummation.

They make their vow complete by making love, which makes new life; thus children give "effect" to their "wishful vow." In this way, their union's fleeting "snatches of delight" betoken the "lasting happiness" of a "large posterity." Their commitment, like its living "fruit," is therefore "endless." And for the endless strength to match it, the groom bids Juno, upholder of the "laws of wedlock," to "bind" his marriage—bind, not bend, for marriage is a *natural* bond that society or religion can only "solemnize."

Since everyone has a stake in his marriage, the groom calls the whole world—even the whole cosmos—as witness. He calls first on the muses in true Renaissance fashion, and then on the maidens attending to his bride; and on all the village boys, too, running and cheering down the streets. The "young men of the town" he bids to light bonfires and "dance about them, and about them sing." To the nymphs of the Irish rivers he calls, and to the fish that teem within. The woods, the moon, and the sun are his witnesses, and even the "heavens, the temple of the gods."[1]

o   o   o

Fast-forward now to the fall of 2006. John Partilla, an Upper West Side advertising executive, meets Carol Anne Riddell, a local news anchor. Like-minded and both brimming with energy, they hit it off; within five years, they are exchanging vows. But when the *New York Times* gives feature coverage to their wedding, it sparks a blaze of controversy.

Partilla and Riddell were married to others when they met—at their children's pre-kindergarten class. In fact, their families had become friends and even vacationed together. But rather than "deny their feelings and live dishonestly," they chose to abandon their spouses and children: "All they had were their feelings, which Ms. Riddell described as 'unconditional and all-encompassing. . . . It was a gift . . . but I had to earn it. Were we brave enough to hold hands and jump?' "

o   o   o

Like "Epithalamion," the *Times* wedding profile embodies a certain view of marriage. Both views are at stake in our national marriage debate.

Spenser's wedding poem sings of an ideal. Translating poetry into prose, we might say that it sees marriage as a *comprehensive* union: Joining spouses in body as well as in mind, it is begun by consent and sealed by sexual intercourse. So completed in the acts of bodily union by which new life is made, it is especially apt for and deepened by procreation, and calls for that broad sharing of domestic life uniquely fit for family life. Uniting spouses in these all-encompassing ways, it also objectively calls for all-encompassing commitment: permanent and exclusive. Comprehensive union is valuable in itself, but its link to children's welfare makes marriage a public good that the state should recognize and support.[2] We call this the *conjugal view* of marriage.

The Partilla-Riddell wedding story may not be poetry, but as a feature article in the much-vied-for Styles section of the world's most famous paper, it too expresses the extreme of a prominent pattern. It sees marriage as the union of two people who commit to romantic partnership and domestic life: essentially an emotional union, merely enhanced by whatever sexual activity the partners find agreeable. Such committed romantic unions are seen as valuable while the emotion lasts. The state recognizes them because it has an interest in their stability, and in the needs of spouses and any children they choose to rear.[3] We call this the *revisionist view* of marriage.

As the Partilla-Riddell story makes clear, there is nothing specifically homosexual about the revisionist view of marriage. It informs many male-female relationships. But it brooks no real difference between these and same-sex relationships: both involve intense emotional union, so both can make a marriage. Comprehensive union, by contrast, is something only a man and woman can form.

Enacting same-sex civil marriage would therefore not be an expansion of the institution of marriage, but a redefinition. Finishing what policies like "no-fault" divorce began, and thus entrenching them, it would finally replace the conjugal view with the revisionist view, elevating the latter to the dignity of legal principle. In so doing, it would multiply the marriage revolution's moral and cultural spoils, and make them harder than ever to recover. Or so we shall argue.

WHY THIS BOOK NOW

In just a few years, this battle over marriage has engaged every branch and level of American government and the whole of our civil society. We have seen executive signings, vetoes, and enforcement decisions; state and federal bills pending and passed; court battles over those decisions and bills; popular referenda in about two-thirds of our states; and debates (or at least position-taking) within academia, professional associations, the media, religious communities, and living rooms across the country. It is hard to think of a more salient cultural conflict.

Same-sex civil marriage finds overwhelming support among intellectuals, journalists, and entertainers, indeed nearly all of our cultural elite. Overall, however, the American people remain unconvinced of its merits. In thirty-two states where the issue has been put to the people in a referendum—including liberal states such as California, Wisconsin, and Maine—the conjugal view of marriage has prevailed. In most of these states, the people have enacted that view constitutionally. Another twelve states have passed statutes doing the same. All told, the people of forty-four states have affirmed the conjugal view of marriage by direct voting or through their representatives.

In six states and the District of Columbia, civil marriage has been redefined to include same-sex relationships. In Massachusetts, Connecticut, and Iowa, this happened by judicial decree; in Vermont, New Hampshire, Washington, D.C., New York, and Maryland by legislation. (As of this writing, Washington State has also passed a same-sex civil marriage bill, to take effect only if upheld in a 2012 referendum.) However this piecemeal battle continues, the record so far explodes the idea that this debate is over, that blind forces of history have somehow fixed a revisionist victory.

While most victories for same-sex civil marriage have come from the bench, courts have upheld conjugal marriage laws more often than not: at least ten state and federal courts have done so in the last decade. But a few pending cases might be the most consequential. One centers on the federal Defense of Marriage Act (DOMA), which defines marriage as a union of man and woman for federal purposes and allows states to choose whether to recognize same-sex marriages contracted elsewhere. Passed overwhelmingly by Congress and signed by President Clinton in 1996, DOMA was declared unconstitutional in 2010 by a federal district court judge in Massachusetts and in 2012 by the First Circuit Court of Appeals. As of this writing, the case has been appealed to the Supreme Court. President Obama, having judged parts of DOMA unconstitutional, has instructed his Department of Justice not to defend it.

Perhaps the most prominent judicial battle is *Hollingsworth v. Perry*. In 2008, after the California Supreme Court had declared California's conjugal marriage law unconstitutional, California voters amended their state constitution to declare marriage a male-female union, leaving intact civil-union laws that granted same-sex relationships all the legal benefits of marriage. In August 2010, a federal court declared Proposition 8 a violation of rights to equal protection and due process under the U.S. Constitution; in 2012, a three-judge panel on the Ninth Circuit affirmed. *Perry* has been appealed to the Supreme Court. There, just five justices might well decide marriage policy for the nation, drawing all these battles to an undemocratically abrupt close. By the Court's standards, marriage laws are constitutional if they have a rational basis. Showing that conjugal marriage laws are indeed rationally grounded is a central purpose of this book. But we hope that it serves mainly as grist for democratic deliberation.

WHAT WE WILL SHOW

Our essential claims may be put succinctly. There is a distinct form of personal union and corresponding way of life, historically called marriage, whose basic features do not depend on the preferences of individuals or cultures. Marriage is, of its essence, a comprehensive union: a union of will (by consent) and body (by sexual union); inherently ordered to procreation and thus the broad sharing of family life; and calling for permanent and exclusive commitment, whatever the spouses' preferences. It has long been and remains a personal and social reality, sought and prized by individuals, couples, and whole societies. But it is also a moral reality: a human good with an objective structure, which it is inherently good for us to live out.

Marriages have always been the main and most effective means of rearing healthy, happy, and well-integrated children. The health and order of society depend on the rearing of healthy, happy, and well-integrated children. That is why law, though it may take no notice of ordinary friendships, should recognize and support marriages.

There can thus be no right for nonmarital relationships to be recognized *as marriages*. There can indeed be much harm, if recognizing them would obscure the shape, and so weaken the special norms, of an institution on which social order depends. So it is not the conferral of benefits on same-sex relationships itself but *redefining marriage in the public mind* that bodes ill for the common good. Indeed, societies mindful of this fact need deprive no same-sex-attracted people of practical goods, social equality, or personal fulfillment.

o   o   o

Here, then, is the heart of our argument against redefinition. If the law defines marriage to include same-sex partners, many will come to misunderstand marriage. They will not see it as essentially comprehensive, or thus (among other things) as ordered to procreation and family life—but as essentially an emotional union. For reasons to be explained, they will therefore tend not to understand or respect the objective norms of permanence or sexual exclusivity that shape it. Nor, in the end, will they see why the terms of marriage should not depend altogether on the will of the parties, be they two or ten in number, as the terms of friendships and contracts do. That is, to the extent that marriage is misunderstood, it will be harder to see the point of its norms, to live by them, and to urge them on others. And this, besides making any remaining restrictions on marriage arbitrary, will damage the many cultural and political goods that get the state involved in marriage in the first place. We list them in summary form here to orient readers. Each will be discussed, and its connection to marriage policy defended, in subsequent chapters of this book.

Real marital fulfillment. No one deliberates or acts in a vacuum. We all take cues from cultural norms, which are shaped by the law. To form a true marriage, one must freely choose it. And to choose marriage, one must have at least a rough, intuitive idea of what it is. The revisionist proposal would harm people (especially future generations) by warping their idea of what marriage is. It would teach that marriage is about emotional union and cohabitation, without any inherent connections to bodily union or family life. As people internalized this view, their ability to realize genuine marital union would diminish. This would be bad in itself, since marital union is good in itself. It would be the subtlest but also the primary harm of redefinition; other harms would be the *effects* of misconstruing marriage, and so not living it out and supporting it.

Spousal well-being. Marriage tends to make spouses healthier, happier, and wealthier than they would otherwise be. But what does this is *marriage*, especially through its distinctive norms of permanence, exclusivity, and orientation to family life. As the state's redefinition of marriage makes these norms harder to understand, cherish, justify, and live by, spouses will benefit less from the psychological and material advantages of marital stability.

Child well-being. If same-sex relationships are recognized as marriages, not only will the norms that keep marriage stable be undermined, but the notion that men and women bring different gifts to parenting will not be reinforced by any civil institution. Redefining marriage would thus soften the social pressures and lower the incentives—already diminished these last few decades—for husbands to stay with their wives and children, or for men and women to marry before having children. All this would harm children's development into happy, productive, upright adults.

Friendship. Misunderstandings about marriage will also speed our society's drought of deep friendship, with special harm to the unmarried. The state will have defined marriage mainly by *degree* or *intensity*—as offering the most of what makes any relationship valuable: shared emotion and experience. It will thus become less acceptable to seek (and harder to find) emotional and spiritual intimacy in nonmarital friendships. These will come to be seen not as different from marriage (and thus distinctively appealing), but simply as *less*. Only the conjugal view gives marriage a definite orientation to bodily union and family life. Only the conjugal view preserves a richly populated horizon with space for many types of communion, each with its own scale of depth and specific forms of presence and care.

Religious liberty. As the conjugal view comes to be seen as irrational, people's freedom to express and live by it will be curbed. Thus, for example, several states have forced Catholic Charities to give up its adoption services or place children with same-sex partners, against Catholic principles. Some conjugal marriage supporters have been fired for publicizing their views. If civil marriage is redefined, believing what virtually every human society once believed about marriage—that it is a male-female union—will be seen increasingly as a malicious prejudice, to be driven to the margins of culture.

Limited government. The state is (or should be) a supporting actor in our lives, not a protagonist. It exists to create the conditions under which we and our freely formed communities can thrive. The most important free community, on which all others depend, is marriage; and the conditions for its thriving include both the accommodations for couples and the pressures on them to stay together that marriage law provides. Redefining civil marriage will further erode marital norms, thrusting the state even more deeply into leading roles for which it is poorly suited: parent and discipliner to the orphaned, provider to the neglected, and arbiter of disputes over custody, paternity, and visitations. As the family weakens, our welfare and correctional bureaucracies grow.

These, in brief, are our main claims, to be elaborated and defended. To opinion leaders, we offer this book as a resource to draw on, or a challenge to meet; and to teachers and students of every persuasion, we offer it as material for analysis, defense, and critique. We offer it to religious bodies considering whether to reform or defend their traditions' teachings on marriage. Finally, since marriage is a good that must be chosen to be realized—and must be roughly understood to be chosen—we offer it to current and future spouses, and to all who witness and support their vows.

WHAT OUR ARGUMENT IS NOT

Before we continue, we should clarify what our argument is *not*. First, it is in the end not about homosexuality. We do not address the morality of homosexual acts or their heterosexual counterparts. We will show that one can defend the conjugal view of marriage while bracketing this moral question and that the conjugal view can be wholeheartedly embraced without denigrating same-sex-attracted people, or ignoring their needs, or assuming that their desires could change. After all, the conjugal view is serenely embraced by many thoughtful people who are same-sex-attracted.[4] Again, this is fundamentally a debate about what marriage is, not about homosexuality.

Second, our argument makes no appeal to divine revelation or religious authority. We think it right and proper to make religious arguments *for or against* a marriage policy (or policies on capital punishment, say, or immigration), but we offer no religious arguments here.

There is simple and decisive evidence that the conjugal view is not peculiar to religion, or to any religious tradition. Ancient thinkers who had no contact with religions such as Judaism or Christianity—including Xenophanes, Socrates, Plato, Aristotle, Musonius Rufus, and Plutarch—reached remarkably similar views of marriage. To be sure, the world's major religions have also historically seen marriage as a conjugal relationship, shaped by its social role in binding men to women and both to the children born of their union. But this suggests only that no one religion invented marriage. It is rather marriage—the demands of a natural institution—that has helped to shape our religious and philosophical traditions.

Third, both social science and history play merely supporting roles in our argument. Children's need for intact families, amply confirmed by social science, is the hook that pulls the law into regulating marriage in the first place. But once the state decides to recognize marriage at all, it is obligated to get marriage *right*, so as to avoid obscuring its distinctive structure and value. Our argument for that structure and value is mainly philosophical, and merely supported by social science at two points: First, the outcomes of different parenting arrangements tend to support our argument that a man and woman's sexual relationship is specially related to rearing children. Second, the practices of different kinds of relationships support our argument that male-female unions call for permanent and exclusive commitment—that there is a rational basis for these norms, quite apart from the spouses' preferences—in a way that isn't true of other bonds.

As for history, we reject the argument that marriage should be opposite-sex because it always was. From a thousand facts about how marriage has been, one can deduce nothing about how it should be. We cite historical support rather to show that the conjugal view of marriage is not uniquely Jewish or Christian; something quite similar to it was developed apart from these traditions.

But history also shows that hostility to homosexually inclined people could not possibly have given rise to the conjugal view. The philosophical and legal principle that only coitus could consummate a marriage arose centuries before the concept of a gay identity, when the only other acts being considered were ones between a married man and woman. And even in cultures very favorable to homoerotic relationships (as in ancient Greece), something akin to the conjugal view has prevailed—and nothing like same-sex marriage was even imagined.

Unavoidably, our argument is complex. As with most important public matters, this debate calls for the close attention and considered judgment of responsible citizens. Though the structure of a universal human good is, in a sense, a simple matter, the simplest things in *this* sense are often the hardest to prove: *Because* the conjugal view has not for many centuries been seriously questioned, defenses of it do not sound common or routine. And because the connection between marriage and sexual complementarity is so foundational, defending it requires drawing extensive connections to other basic principles of marriage, as we do below. We will show, in other words, that the conjugal view better explains what most agree are integral features of marriage, and that it better explains their unity.

Finally, we recognize that some, having simply dismissed our view as a noxious mix of obscurantism and bigotry, will be unwilling—perhaps unable—to entertain defenses of it. We harbor no illusions that those committed to shielding their ears from reasonable arguments will be reached by a book that aims to offer reasonable arguments. We see the marriage debate as one between people of sound mind and character who disagree on the solution to what they agree is a debate worth having. Our book is addressed to revisionists who see it likewise.

§ 1 §

Challenges to Revisionists

FOR ALL THE DIFFICULTY AND AMBIGUITY OF MAKING value judgments, the broadest outlines of the good life are plain to most of us. One man has a healthy body and a happy family, an enriching complement of hobbies, and a keen sense for Bob Dylan. By day he teaches high-school seniors to savor the rhythm and wit of Chaucer's poetry; by night friends help him savor red Bordeaux. A second man is debilitated, depressed, desensitized, and detached. It does not take a poet or a saint to see who is better off.

It is equally clear that there is nothing special about Dylan, Chaucer, or Bordeaux that gives the first man his advantage. There is no *single* good life, but a range of good lives: countless ways of blending the basic ingredients of human thriving. But the ingredients themselves—the most foundational ways in which we can thrive, what we might call "basic human goods"—are more limited. These are the conditions or activities that in themselves make us better off, whether or not they bring us other goods. It makes sense for us to want these for their *own* sake. Health, knowledge, play, and aesthetic delight are a few examples, and another is friendship.

Yet another basic human good, we think, is marriage. A critical point here is that marriage and ordinary friendship do not simply offer different degrees of the same type of human good, like two checks written in different amounts. Nor are they simply varieties of the same good, like the enjoyment of a Matisse and the enjoyment of a Van Gogh. Each is its own kind of good, a way of thriving that is different in kind from the other. Hence, while spouses should be friends, what it takes to be a good friend is not just the same as what it takes to be a good spouse.

What, then, is distinctive about marriage? All sorts of practices are grafted onto marriage by law and custom, but what kind of relationship *must any* two people have to enjoy the specific good of marriage? This framing of the question, though unusual, should not seem mysterious; we could ask it just as well of other basic human goods.

Friendship, for instance, has an objective core. Suppose someone thought that friendship was mainly about people using each other, with occasional good will and cooperation just an optional spice. Most of us would consider him mistaken about what real friendship is. He would not just be mistaken about the meaning of a *word* ("friendship") as we happen to use it. He would be mistaken about a universal fact: a basic human good, one of the core ways of *being well*. Or if, as often happens, a student seemed to think and live as if the good of knowledge amounted to the ability to use long and impressive words, we would consider him lacking in a dimension of human well-being—not just in the proper use of the term "knowledge."

So, too, with marriage. We will argue that those seeking to redefine civil marriage misunderstand a human good—not just a legal artifact or title. The more people internalize this misunderstanding of marriage, the less positioned they are to live out the real thing. The question then remains: what *is* marriage?

We begin by showing in this chapter why, whatever else is true, the revisionist view must be *false*: wrong about marriage. Its deep errors are often overlooked, on the implicit assumption that if the conjugal view is wrong, revisionism must be right. This is obviously mistaken logic and, in fact, the revisionist view fails on its own terms: no coherent version of it can account for three points common to both sides of the debate: the state has an interest in regulating certain relationships; that interest exists only if the relationships are sexual; and it exists only if they are monogamous.

In short, the revisionist view sees your spouse as your "Number One person," in one advocate's pithy phrase.[1] Hence it cannot distinguish marriage from simple companionship. And we all know that companionship, while deeply enriching, is far more general than marriage.[2] So this objection, if sound, should be disqualifying. Yet it has been leveled for years without a single good answer, and is amply confirmed by revisionists' own rhetoric and the policies that they ultimately come to support.

THE STATE HAS AN INTEREST IN REGULATING SOME RELATIONSHIPS?

Imagine a world in which the law set the terms of your ordinary friendships: You and a coworker could not strike up a friendship across cubicles without first getting the state's approval, which it could deny you for being too young or otherwise unqualified. Having formed a friendship, you could not end it without the state's permission. You could even be forced to pay for projects once pursued with estranged friends—until your death, and under threat of imprisonment.

This would be madness, and we all see why: ordinary friendships simply do not affect the common good in structured ways that could justify legal regulation. Why, then, do we—and every culture we know—legally regulate marriage?

We all have an interest in our neighbors' marriages that we do not have in their friendships, and marriages have a definite structure that friendships lack.[3] As we will argue in chapter 3, societies rely on families built on strong marriages to produce what they need but cannot secure: healthy, upright children who become conscientious citizens. As they mature, children benefit from the love and care of both mother and father, and from their parents' committed and exclusive love for each other. Unlike friendships, which vary in kind and degree and formality, marriage—we will show—has enough *objective* structure, apart from spouses' preferences, to be legally regulated.

The revisionist view severs this important link. If marriage is centrally an emotional union, rather than one inherently ordered to family life, it becomes much harder to show why the state should concern itself with marriage any more than with friendship. Why involve the state in what amounts to the legal regulation of tenderness? The revisionist proposes a policy that she cannot give reasons for enacting.

ONLY IF THEY ARE SEXUAL?

Some argue simply that the state should grant people certain legal benefits if they provide one another with domestic support and care. But such a scheme would not be marriage, nor could it make sense of the features of marriage law.

Take Oscar and Alfred. They live together, support each other, share domestic responsibilities, and have no dependents. Because Oscar knows and trusts Alfred more than anyone else, he would like Alfred to be the one to visit him in the hospital if he is ill, give directives for his care if he is unconscious, and inherit his assets if he dies first. Alfred feels the same about Oscar. Each offers the other security amid life's hardships, and company in its victories. They face the world together.

So far, you may be assuming that Oscar and Alfred have a sexual relationship. But does it matter? What if they are bachelor brothers? What if they are college best friends who never stopped rooming together, or who reunited as widowers? In these cases, most agree, they would not be spouses. And yet they would be, by most revisionists' arguments.

Assuming a general policy of recognizing committed dyads, should the benefits that Oscar and Alfred receive depend on whether their relationship is or can be presumed to be sexual? Would it not be patently *unjust* if the state withheld benefits from them only because they were not having sex with each other? A Syracuse Law professor has argued that it would be: that the state should recognize social units made up of committed friends.[4]

The revisionist cannot successfully answer by claiming that marriages are the most emotionally intense of relationships, and that sex generally fosters and expresses that intimacy. Emotional bonds are certainly important, especially in marriage. But if sex matters for marriage only for its emotional and expressive effects, as the revisionist must hold, then surely sex is perfectly replaceable, as no one really holds. Emotional intimacy is also fostered by deep conversation, cooperation under pressure or imminent tragedy, and a thousand other activities that two sisters or a father and son could choose without raising an eyebrow. There is nothing in *this* respect unique to sex.

In other words, *why* is sex more expressive of marriage than other pleasing activities that build attachment? We know that passion, pleasure, and delight in any genuine good, including marital union, are themselves also valuable; emotional union is an important part of marital union. But if spraying oxytocin at your partner increased her pleasure and attachment to you, that would not make it fungible with sex as an embodiment of your marriage. But *why* not, unless something about sex besides its emotional effects is *also* crucial? In the next chapter, we will show that only the conjugal view can answer this question. For it can show how the sort of sexual union made possible by sexual complementarity creates more than merely emotional union, as marriage requires.

You might reply, "People in love naturally seek sex and commitment, and then we call them 'married.' What's to explain?" But this misses the point: What is so different about sex that it can set a class of bonds apart—not just in name or feelings, but in the type of value realized and commitment involved—from the spectrum of *non-sexual* bonds compatible with *various* commitments? What *unifies* sex and the other features of marriage as one good? The answer, we argue below, is this: Marriage essentially involves all-encompassing—including bodily—union, and sex unites bodily as no other activity can. But as we also show, sex that unites in this sense—making two people one, much as parts of a single body are one—requires a man and a woman.

ONLY IF THEY ARE MONOGAMOUS?

Now take the example of Oscar and Alfred and add Herman to the mix. To filter out the argument about sexual union, assume that the three men are in a romantic triad, like one just profiled sympathetically in *New York Magazine*.[5] Does anything change? If one dies, the other two are coheirs. If one is ill, either of the others can visit or give directives. If Oscar and Alfred could have their romantic relationship recognized, why not Oscar, Alfred, and Herman? Why is it not invidious discrimination to deny the state's recognition to *their* relationship of mutual care and affection?

For revisionists, marriage must be distinguished simply by emotional union and the activities that foster it. But why should *these* be limited to two people? Indeed, *how* could they be, if we form emotional connections with various loved ones— parents, siblings, close friends—and by various activities? Romantic emotional unions do have a different quality from others and are clearly important for marriage, but emotional hues are hardly *enough* to mark the difference in kind between marriage and ordinary forms of friendship.* Moreover, we cannot directly control emotions, so they are unlikely candidates for the central object of a vow. And if some relationships turn out, as sometimes reported, *more* stable or emotionally fulfilling when

---

*As we discuss in the next chapter, community is built by common action toward common goods. So we can distinguish types of bonds not simply by feelings, but by the kinds of cooperation they involve and the goods to which they are ordered. We will argue that any coherent way of explaining what sets marriage apart in these ways also shows that marriage requires a man and a woman.

sexually open, and marriage is emotional union, how could exclusivity be integral to it? Nor can the revisionist defend exclusivity by pointing out that people in love usually desire it: people in love usually desire the opposite sex, too, and many in polyamorous unions see specific emotional benefits in the sexual variety and suppression of jealousy that multiple-partner unions involve.[6] They may think that single- and multiple-partner relationships just offer different costs and benefits. Why, then, can only two make a marriage?

Some might object that everyone just knows this. It requires no explanation. But this begs the question against Oscar, Alfred, and Herman, who want social recognition of the kind of relationship that they find most personally fulfilling, and its advantages: economic benefits, legal protections, and freedom from stigma for themselves and their children.

As chapter 2 will show, the conjugal view explains why marriage is possible only between two people. It also makes clear *how* spousal commitment can be exclusive. Since it sees marriage as something more specific than emotional union, which other activities promote to some degree and which sexual exclusivity might sometimes seem to *diminish*, the conjugal view alone can justify drawing a bright line around sexual activity as the behavior that spouses must pledge to share only with each other. Only the conjugal view can justify such extensive commitment as the norm for marriage.

The revisionist's difficulty linking sex and marriage, or marriage and exclusivity, also arises for marriage and family life. If rearing children might hamper as well as help emotional attachment, how can revisionists explain the fact that family life by its nature enriches marriage, but only marriage? That rearing children is more deeply linked to marriage than any other kind of bond, even other stable ones that might sometimes involve childrearing in practice (as between, say, widowed cohabiting sisters)? This, too, only the conjugal view can explain.

Can revisionists explain *any* systematic difference between marriage and deep friendship?

o   o   o

Before we show how the conjugal view can, a brief note. Many who encounter these objections to the revisionist view react by trying to dismiss them. They suggest, for example, that no one is clamoring for recognition of polyamorous unions, or that we are invoking a "slippery slope" argument.

Note first that there is nothing wrong with arguing against a policy based on reasonable predictions of unwanted consequences. Such predictions would seem quite reasonable in this case, given that prominent figures such as feminist icon Gloria Steinem, political activist and author Barbara Ehrenreich, and New York University Law Professor Kenji Yoshino have already demanded legal recognition of multiple-partner sexual relationships.[7] Nor are such relationships unheard of: *Newsweek* reports that there are more than five hundred thousand in the United States alone.[8] In Brazil, a public notary has recognized a trio as a civil union.[9] Mexico City has considered expressly temporary marriage licenses.[10] The Toronto District School Board has taken to promoting polyamorous relationships among its students.[11] We could go on.

Still, here we are not predicting the social or legal consequences of the revisionist view. We are trying to drive home a different point: if you insist as a matter of *principle* that we should recognize same-sex relationships as marriages, the same principle will require you to accept (and favor legally recognizing) polyamorous—and, as we saw above, nonsexual—relationships as marriages. If you think conjugal marriage laws unjustly discriminate against same-sex relationships, you will have no way of showing why the same is not true of multiple-partner and nonsexual ones.

In other words, on the best accounts on which two men or two women can marry, marriage consists of emotional union and domestic life. But as pleasing and valuable as emotional union can be, there's nothing about marriage *so* understood that also requires it to be dyadic, sexually closed, or even sexual at all. Yet bonds that lack these features just aren't marriages. So the best theories by which any two men or women can marry are mistaken: they get other, less disputed aspects of marriage wrong.

Elizabeth Brake embraces the first horn of this dilemma with gusto. She supports "minimal marriage," in which "individuals can have legal marital relationships with more than one person, reciprocally or asymmetrically, themselves determining the sex and number of parties, the type of relationship involved, and which rights and responsibilities to exchange with each."[12] But Brake purchases this consistency at a high cost. The more that the parties to a "minimal marriage" determine case-by-case which duties to exchange, the less the proposed marriage policy itself accomplishes in a world where private contracts are already available. As we deprive marriage policy of definite shape, we deprive it of public purpose.

Rigorously pursued, the logic of rejecting the conjugal conception of marriage thus leads, by way of formlessness, toward pointlessness: it proposes a policy for which it can hardly explain the benefit. Of course, some revisionists will defend their preferred norms as simply the most workable or the most likely to have the best consequences. We address them elsewhere (see chapters 3, 4, and 6). Most revisionists, however, support norms like exclusivity as a matter of principle. But they have not succeeded when challenged to explain the basis of these norms.[13] This is no fault of theirs, but of their position: it has no coherent defense.

❧ 2 ❧

Comprehensive Union

WHAT, THEN, *IS* MARRIAGE? AS ITS TITLE SUGGESTS, THIS book provides our answer. More succinctly, so does this sentence: Marriage is a comprehensive union of persons. Let us explain.

It is impossible for two people to be one, or united, in *every* sense without ceasing to be two people. So unity of that sort is not even desirable. Marriage is not comprehensive in *that* sense. Good spouses need not hold the same jobs or play the same musical instruments. But any kind of community is formed by consent to pursuing certain goods and by certain activities, following the commitment appropriate to those activities and goods. It is in those three basic features of any bond—unifying activity, unifying goods, and unifying commitment—that marriage is comprehensive.

First, it unites two people in their most basic dimensions, in their minds *and* bodies; second, it unites them with respect to procreation, family life, and its broad domestic sharing; and third, it unites them permanently and exclusively.

COMPREHENSIVE UNIFYING ACTS:
MIND *AND* BODY

First, unlike ordinary friendship, marriage unites people in all their basic dimensions. It involves a union of minds and wills that unfolds in a sharing of lives and resources. But marriage also includes bodily union. This is because your body is an essential part of *you*, not a vehicle driven by the "real" you, your mind; nor a mere costume you must don. If a man ruins your car, he vandalizes your property, but if he slices your leg, he injures *you*. Since the body is part of the human person, there is a difference in kind between vandalism and violation; between destruction of property and mutilation of bodies.

This point has been developed at length.[1] But we can make it vivid by considering some of its other moral implications: What is *peculiarly* perverse about torture? That it uses some aspects of a *person* (body and affects) against other aspects of his or her self (wishes, choices, and commitments). Why is rape gravely wicked even when performed on someone in a coma who never finds out and sustains no lasting injuries? It still involves misusing—abusing—a *person*, and not merely using and replacing intact his or her property. More positively, spouses find it beautiful and uniquely appropriate that their children are a mixture of their bodies. Couples see their infertility as a tragic limitation even when they can adopt. Proud new parents care which child is handed to them in the maternity ward. The evidence of our embodiedness, and of its value, is all around us.

Because of that embodiedness, any union of two people *must include bodily union* to be comprehensive. If it did not, it would leave out—it would fail to be extended along—a basic part of each person's being.[2]

Suppose a man and woman build an exclusive relationship based on deep conversation. They pledge to talk about their most secret sorrows and joys with each other, and only each other, until death do them part. Have they married? Clearly not. If we substitute for deep conversation some more overtly physical act—besides sex—they still are not married. Marriage requires exclusivity with respect to *sex*, to a certain kind of *bodily union*. But what makes sex special? Our bodies can touch and interact in all sorts of ways, so why can sexual union make two people one body ("one flesh," to cite ancient Hebrew scripture, and a concept central to many legal and philosophical traditions about marriage) as nothing else can?[3]

Start with a more familiar case. Something about your organs—your heart, stomach, lungs—makes *them* one body, one organic substance. But what? It is not that they are together in space: rocks in a pile do not make one mineral substance. Nor is it their shared genetic code: Identical twins have (roughly) one code but not one body; a transplant patient's heart is part of his body, but differently coded.

No, what makes for unity is common action: activity toward common ends. Two things are parts of a greater whole—*are one* —if they *act as one*; and they act as one if they coordinate *toward one end that encompasses them both*. A carburetor on a Detroit assembly line and a transmission in Highland Park are two things; when combined to coordinate toward a single encompassing goal (convenient locomotion), they form one machine: say, a Model T.

Organic unity is similar, only stronger: Henry Ford's design —a human *choice*—imposed unity on the parts of the Model T. The parts of a body have their unity by *nature*. They are *naturally* incomplete when apart, *naturally* greater than their sum when together.

In short, then, your organs are one body because they are coordinated for a single *biological* purpose of the whole that they form together: sustaining your biological life. Just so, for two individuals to unite organically, *their bodies must coordinate toward a common biological end of the whole that they form together.* When they do so, they do not just touch or interlock. Their union is not just felt, or metaphorical (see appendix). Though more limited, it is as real as the union of a single body's parts.

Between two people, that sort of union is impossible through functions like digestion, for which individuals are naturally sufficient. But it is a remarkable fact that there is one respect in which this highest kind of bodily unity *is* possible between two individuals, one function for which a mate really does *complete* us: sexual reproduction. In coitus, and there alone, a man and a woman's bodies participate by virtue of their sexual complementarity in a coordination that has the biological purpose of reproduction—a function that neither can perform alone. Their coordinated action is, biologically, the first step (the behavioral part) of the reproductive process. By engaging in it, they are united, and do not merely touch, much as one's heart, lungs, and other organs are united: by coordinating toward a biological good of the whole that they form together. Here the whole is the couple; the single biological good, their reproduction.*

But bodily coordination is possible even when its end is not realized; so for a couple, bodily union occurs in coitus even when conception does not. It is the *coordination toward a single end* that makes the union; achieving the end would deepen the union but is not necessary for it.

This means that there is something special about the *sort* of act that causes conception: coitus. Our legal and philosophical traditions have, significantly, long termed this act the *generative* act.[4] If (and only if) coitus is a free and loving expression of the spouses' commitment, then it is also a *marital* act. In other words, the marital act involves the most distinctively marital *behavior* (bodily union in coitus), chosen for distinctively marital *reasons*: to make spousal love concrete, to unite as spouses

---

*We nowhere rely on the "perverted faculty argument," which says that it is wrong to use organs against their natural purposes. We consider this argument fallacious.

do, to extend their union of hearts and minds onto the bodily plane.*

All interpersonal unions are, so far as they go, valuable in themselves: not just as a means to other ends. So a husband and wife's loving bodily union in coitus and the special kind of relationship that it seals are valuable, even when conception is neither sought nor achieved. But two men, two women, and larger groups cannot achieve organic bodily union: there is no bodily good or function toward which their bodies can coordinate.

In particular, pleasure—say, as a means to deeper attachment —cannot play this role for several reasons. The good must be truly common and for the couple as a whole, but mental states are private and benefit partners, if at all, only individually. The good must be bodily, but pleasures as such are aspects of experience. The good must be inherently valuable, but pleasures are good in themselves only when they are taken in some other, independent good.[5] So while pleasure and delight deepen and enrich a marital union where one exists, they cannot be its foundation. They cannot stand on their own.

---

*Criticizing our argument, Jason Lee Steorts scoffed at the implication that "the value of a relationship between two persons in love [would depend] on the structure of their genitals." But one might as well ridicule the idea that Juliet's attraction to Romeo could depend "on the structure of Romeo's genitals." Similarly, people often ask scornfully what could be so special about penile-vaginal intercourse. But one could ask of the revisionist what's so special about bonds enhanced by orgasm. With the right (unfair) description, any view can be ridiculed. The question is not whether there's a description that obscures the special value of conjugal acts, but whether there is a true description that highlights it. *Organic bodily union* and *life-giving act*, both related to the concept of *comprehensive union*, make the special value of marriage luminous, but apply only to husband and wife. See Jason Lee Steorts, "Two Views of Marriage, and the Falsity of the Choice between Them," *National Review*, February 7, 2011, http://www.national review.com/articles/263672/two-views-marriage-and-falsity-choice-between -them-jason-lee-steorts. For a reply, see Sherif Girgis, "Real Marriage," *National Review*, March 21, 2011, http://www.nationalreview.com/articles/263679/real -marriage-sherif-girgis.

Only bodily coordination toward reproduction, then, gives rise to organic bodily union. Whether other acts are good, bad, or indifferent, they bring about no true bodily union. So the relationships that they are meant to foster, good or bad, cannot be marital: for marital means comprehensive, and comprehensive includes bodily.

COMPREHENSIVE UNIFYING GOODS: PROCREATION AND DOMESTIC LIFE

Second, besides uniting spouses in every basic dimension (body and mind), marriage unites them in pursuit of every basic kind of good. In particular, marriage calls for the wide-ranging cooperation of a shared domestic life, for it is uniquely ordered to having and rearing children:* The comprehensive *good* of family life enriches a marriage as such, and lack of children is a lack for a marriage, in a way that is not true for best friends, roommates, or teammates. Most people acknowledge this fact about marriage. The conjugal view best explains it.

By "shared domestic life" we mean more than the courteous noninterference that two mismatched freshman roommates might achieve by winter break. Spouses unite the whole of their selves (mind and body), and the demands of marriage are shaped by those of parenting. So marriage requires coordination (compatibility) of the whole of the spouses' lives, as well as some positive cooperation in the major dimensions of human development, which are, after all, the major dimensions of child development: physical, intellectual, social, moral, aesthetic, and so on. In all these ways, again, the goods to which marriage is aimed are comprehensive.

But once we've defined it, we can see that shared domestic life would be at best an optional bonus, and at worst a suffocat-

---

*This point, often misunderstood, is worth clarifying. It is not that only true spouses could want, decide, or manage to rear children together. The point is that even apart from people's decisions and desires, marriage is the kind of bond inherently fulfilled and extended by the spouses' having and rearing children.

ing hindrance, to nonfamilial bonds, just as surely as rearing a child with your college roommate would be. What, then, *makes* marriage different in these two ways?

Just deciding to rear children is not enough to make you married: three monks who commit to caring for an orphan do not thereby marry. Nor is childrearing *necessary* for being spouses.

Accordingly, our law for centuries has treated coitus, not adoption or birth or conception, as the event that consummates a marriage, and has recognized the marriages of infertile couples.[6] This should not surprise us. The idea that we are trying to explain is *not* that the relationship of marriage and the comprehensive good of rearing children always go together. It is that, like a ball and socket, they *fit* together: that family life specially *enriches* marriage; that marriage is especially *apt* for family life, which shapes its norms.

A more promising way to explain this connection between marriage and family life is to consider how other bonds are specially related to certain goods via certain activities.

Ordinary friendships, for example, are unions of minds and wills, by which each friend comes to know and seek the other's good. So they are sealed—friends are most obviously and truly *befriending*—in conversations and common pursuits. Scholarly relationships are most embodied in joint inquiry, discovery, and publication; drama troupes, in rehearsals and shows. There is a parallel, in other words, between the common good to which any bond is ordered and the activity that most embodies it.

To be clear, it is not just that certain activities *symbolize* the fact that a relationship is of this or that type. They partly *make it so*. A baseball team does not just show the world what it is through practices and games; rather, playing the game is how teammates *make* themselves more truly what they have committed to being together.

So if there is some basic connection between the comprehensive good of procreation (hence family life) and the bond of marriage, we can expect a parallel link between procreation and the activity that enacts, renews, or embodies a marriage.

That connection is obvious if the conjugal view is correct: Procreation is the good that fulfills and extends a marriage, because it fulfills and extends the act that embodies or consummates the commitment of marriage: sexual intercourse, the generative act. Conversely, if a man and woman commit to form the sort of union fulfilled by the good of family life, then coitus—the sort of act fulfilled by conception—uniquely embodies or renews their commitment. It mirrors, at the bodily level, the sort of bond they have established by consent.

In short, marriage is ordered to family life because the act by which spouses make love also makes new life; one and the same act both seals a marriage and brings forth children. That is why marriage alone is the loving union of mind and body fulfilled by the procreation—and rearing—of whole new human beings.

Relationships of two men, two women, or more than two, whatever their moral status, cannot be marriages because they lack this inherent link to procreation. Any sexual acts they involve, in addition to not being organic bodily unions, will not be ordered to procreation; so they will not embody a commitment ordered to family life: a marital commitment. Unsurprisingly, in the common-law tradition, only coitus (not mutual stimulation by other means, even between a legally wedded man and woman) has been recognized as consummating a marriage.

This is not to say that infertile couples cannot marry. Consider again the sports analogy: The kind of cooperation that makes a group into a baseball team is largely aimed at winning games. Teammates develop and share their athletic skills in the way best suited for honorable wins—for example, with assiduous practice and good sportsmanship. But such development and sharing are possible and inherently valuable for teammates even when they do not win a game.

Just so, marital cooperation in both sexual and domestic life is characteristically ordered to procreation and childrearing. Spouses develop and share their whole selves in the way best suited for honorably parenting—for example, with broad domestic sharing and permanent, exclusive commitment. But such development and sharing, including the bodily union of the generative act, are possible and inherently valuable for spouses even when they do not conceive (see chapter 5 on the infertility objection).

Professor Kenji Yoshino objects that this baseball analogy implies that infertile couples are somehow "losers."[7] Of course it implies nothing of the sort; infertility in no way reflects on spouses' efforts or character. But there is no denying what countless infertile couples would be first to admit: Infertility is a *loss*, a regrettable lack. It makes it impossible for the couple's union, though marital, to be in a new and quite literal sense *embodied*.

On the other hand, procreation need not (even where it can) be the most important aspect of a marriage, nor should it be its sole point. Comprehensive union is valuable in itself, distinctly so, and should be treated that way. Treating it as a mere means detracts from spousal love. But here the analogy holds up: winning need not be a team's only goal, and indeed *exclusive* focus on winning can ruin teammates' experience, by detracting from camaraderie and love of the game.

Yet (to juice our analogy to the last), in baseball as in marriage, the end plays a crucial role even when beyond reach: if nine people do not commit to engage in cooperation ordered to winning (say, if they only run laps about the field), they do not realize the specific good of playing ball. They are not a true team. And if two or more people do not commit to engage in cooperation even *ordered*[8] to procreation (coitus), they do not realize the specific good of marriage. Desired or not, achieved or not, procreation and winning each distinguish a practice by shaping some of its activities, activities that give the practice some of its distinctive value.

We can now spell out another unique feature of marriage only briefly noted so far. The sharing of life that most forms of community call for is limited, because the common values that define them are limited. (The bowling league, defined by the sportsmanly quest for skillful performance, may call for regular weekly or monthly attendance, but there is no loss in not *living* with your bowling partner. Domestic sharing between non-spouses, even where possible, is not generally *called for*.) But marriage unites spouses in mind and body, and is ordered to producing not just one or another human value but whole new persons, new centers of value. So it inherently calls for the broad sharing of life that would be needed for helping new human beings develop their capacities for pursuing *every* basic kind of value. That is, spouses benefit as spouses from at least some co-operation intellectually, in recreation, and so on.[9]

What marriage is, and what our marriage policy should be—these are questions about basic values, about what we *ought* to do as a society. So they cannot be settled by the descriptions of social science alone, any more than the moral status of our health care laws can be settled by the cause-and-effect descriptions of pharmacology. We doubt that anyone, on reflection, really denies this: if parenting by four people had the same outcomes as two-person parenting, neither we *nor* revisionists would be forced to deny that marriage calls for monogamy.

At the same time, if parenting (cooperating as mother and father) really does uniquely fulfill marriage, it is natural to expect that marriage is normally apt for parenting. Indeed, as we will see in the next two chapters, according to the best available sociological evidence, children fare best overall when reared by their wedded biological parents. So not only does childrearing deepen and extend a marriage; children also benefit from marriage.

COMPREHENSIVE COMMITMENT: A RATIONAL BASIS FOR NORMS OF PERMANENCE AND EXCLUSIVITY

To recapitulate: marriage involves acts that unite spouses comprehensively, and it unites them in pursuit of a comprehensive range of goods. So, third and finally, in virtue of both these facts, marriage alone *requires* comprehensive commitment, whatever the spouses' preferences.

To become someone's friend, you must be committed to her good and to the friendship. But that commitment need not be very formal or very extensive. Implicit and temporary commitments will do, and exclusive ones are at best unusual. Indeed, they are hard to imagine. If friendship is a union of hearts and minds, if as a category it ranges wildly across a vast spectrum of conversations and ordinary pursuits, is there any definable (not to say healthy and humane) way to be only one person's friend?

But as a union of spouses in mind *and body*, ordered to having and rearing children in the context of broad life sharing, marriage both makes sense of permanent and exclusive commitment, and requires it to get off the ground. Our point here is subtle and sometimes misunderstood: While people in other bonds may wish for, promise, and live out permanent sexual exclusivity, only marriage objectively requires such a commitment if it is to be realized fully. Only in marriage is there a principled basis for these norms apart from what spouses happen to prefer.

Marriage is possible between only two because no act can organically unite three or more, or thus seal a comprehensive union of three or more lives. If bodily union is essential to marriage, we can understand why marriage, like the union of organs into one healthy whole, should be total and lasting for the life of the parts ("till death us do part").[10] Being organically united—as "one flesh"—spouses should have, by *commitment*, the exclusive and lifelong unity that the parts of a healthy organic body have by nature.[11]

Moreover, their mind-body union is ordered to the comprehensive good of rearing new members of the human family— their children—an open-ended task calling for the coordination of their whole lives, which in turn requires undivided commitment. Thus, the norms of marriage, a union specially enriched by family life, fittingly create the stability and harmony suitable for rearing children. Sociology and common sense agree that such stability is undermined by divorce, which deprives children of an intact biological family, and by infidelity—which betrays and divides one's attention to spouse and children, often with children from other couplings.[12] The intrinsic connection between marriage and children therefore reinforces the reasons spouses have to stay together and faithful for life.

In short, a union comprehensive in these senses—a union of mind and body, ordered to procreation and family life—must by the same token be comprehensive in commitment: through time (hence the vow of permanence) and at each time (hence the vow of exclusivity). But in the revisionist account of marriage, where organic bodily union, an orientation to family life, and broad domestic sharing are at best optional, so are permanence and exclusivity.

Finally, the conjugal view better explains why spouses should pledge *sexual* exclusivity at all. If marriage is, as the revisionist must hold, essentially an emotional union, this norm is hard to explain. After all, sex is just one of many pleasing activities that foster vulnerability and tenderness, and some partners might experience deeper and longer-lasting emotional union with each other if their relationship were sexually open. But the conjugal view distinguishes marriage by a certain type of cooperation, defined by certain common ends: bodily union and its natural fulfillment in children and family life. So it is not at all arbitrary in picking out sexual activity as central to the vow of exclusivity.

In nonmarital relationships, again, it is hard to see why this sort of commitment, if it can be specified at all, should be not only desirable whenever not very costly (as stability always is), but *required* for anyone hoping to form such a relationship. This is borne out by reasoned reflection, revisionists' own arguments, the progress of recent policy proposals, and preliminary social science (see chapters 1 and 4).

○   ○   ○

In this chapter we've argued that the conjugal view is the correct view of marriage, understood as a basic human good, a distinctive way of thriving. It remains to argue for preserving this view in the law, and against the objections to doing so. Because these other arguments all depend on the one made here, it is worth closing this chapter with a summary of its central points.

Any kind of voluntary bond begins with people's *consent* to cooperate—to engage in *activities* aimed at certain shared *goods*. These are the activities that most distinctively embody or seal their specific form of relationship, and thus their relationship. The *commitment* governing that relationship—the set of norms that they should pledge to observe—is in turn fixed by, and serves, the relationship's goods and activities.

For example, a scholarly community exists whenever a group of people consents to cooperate in activities ordered toward the good of gaining knowledge (research, publication, etc.). So their specific kind of bond is made concrete and built up—it is made most present and real—whenever they engage in those activities. The norms of academic integrity that they observe as part of their commitment—for example, to disclose all relevant findings, even when inconvenient—are in turn fixed by the demands of knowledge, the aim of research.

Everyone knows that marriage is a kind of relationship. An account of marriage must explain what makes the *marital* relationship different from others. In our view, the kind of union created by consent to *marriage* is uniquely comprehensive in how it unites persons, what it unites them with respect to, and how extensive a commitment it demands.

First, marriage unites persons in their *bodies* as well as their minds. The bodily union of two people is much like the bodily union of organs in an individual. Just as one's organs form a unity by coordinating for the biological good of the whole (one's survival), so the bodies of a man and woman form a unity by coordination (coitus) for a biological good (reproduction) of their union as a whole. In choosing such biological coordination, spouses unite bodily, in a way that has generative significance, and do not merely touch or interlock. This generative kind of act physically embodies their specific, marital commitment.

Also, spouses unite bodily only by coitus, which is ordered toward the good of bringing new human life into the world. New life, in a sense, is one human good among others, but in another sense, it transcends and includes other human goods. Having consented to sharing in the generative acts that unite them organically (as "one flesh"), spouses cooperate in other areas of life (intellectual, recreational, etc.) in the broad domestic sharing uniquely apt for fostering the all-around development of new human beings. Of course, they also cooperate in the tasks of parenting when children do come. Ordinary friendships—the unions of hearts and minds embodied in conversations and various joint pursuits—can have more limited and variable scope.

Finally, in view of its comprehensiveness in these other senses, marriage inherently calls for comprehensive commitment: permanence and exclusivity. Like the union of organs into one healthy whole organism, marriage is properly total and lasting for the life of the parts. (Indeed, comprehensive union can be achieved *only* by two people, because no act can organically unite three or more people bodily.) Again, marriage is uniquely apt for having and rearing children, an inherently open-ended task calling for unconditional commitment. But friendships as such require no promise of permanence and are enhanced, not betrayed, by openness to new members.

In short, as most people acknowledge, marriage involves a bodily as well as mental union of spouses, a special link to children and domestic life, and permanent and exclusive commitment. All three elements converge in, and go to constitute, the conjugal view.

℘ 3 ℘

The State and Marriage

THE CONJUGAL VIEW BETTER DESCRIBES WHAT DISTIN-guishes marriage from other human goods, other ways of thriving—something that the revisionist view is helpless to do. That was the theme of our first two chapters. Like nonmarital friendship, of course, marriage is a type of bond. But marriage is a bond of a special kind. It unites spouses in body as well as mind and heart, and it is especially apt for, and enriched by, procreation and family life. In light of both these facts, it alone objectively calls for commitments of permanence and exclusivity. Spouses vow their *whole* selves for their *whole* lives. This comprehensiveness puts the value of marriage in a class apart from the value of other relationships.

Against this, some on the libertarian Right say that marriage has no *public* value, and call for the state to get out of the marriage business altogether. Voices on the Left say that marriage has no *distinctive* public value; they say the state may work it like clay, remaking marriage to fit our preferences. Here we show where both go wrong.

WHY *CIVIL* MARRIAGE?

The more intimate a relationship, the *less* it tends to attract the state's attention. Business dealings are regulated, but the law does not set terms for our friendships or allow us to sue over their neglect. There are no civil ceremonies for forming friendships or legal obstacles to ending them. Why is marriage different? The answer is that friendship does not affect the common good in structured ways that warrant legal recognition and regulation; marriage does.

This is the only way to account for the remarkable fact that almost all cultures have regulated male-female sexual relationships. These relationships alone produce new human beings. For these new and highly dependent people, there is no path to physical, moral, and cultural maturity without a long and delicate process of ongoing care and supervision—one to which men and women typically bring different strengths, and for which they are better suited the more closely related they are to the children. Unless children do mature, they will never become healthy, upright, productive members of society; and that state of economic and social development we call "civilization" depends on healthy, upright, productive citizens. But regularly producing such citizens is nearly impossible unless men and women commit their lives to each other and any children they might have. So it is a summary, but hardly an exaggeration, to say that civilization depends on strong marriages.

Maggie Gallagher captures this insight with the slogan that "sex makes babies, society needs babies, and children need mothers and fathers." She develops the idea: "The critical public or 'civil' task of marriage is to regulate sexual relationships between men and women in order to reduce the likelihood that children (and their mothers, and society) will face the burdens of fatherlessness, and increase the likelihood that there will be a next generation that will be raised by their mothers and fathers in one family, where both parents are committed to each other and to their children."[1]

Even now, this claim is not partisan. Thus David Blankenhorn, a liberal Democrat:

> If you've been trained, as anthropology field researchers typically are, to begin at the beginning—to start with the most fundamental issues—you will report a cluster of related facts: Humans are social; they live in groups. They strongly seek to reproduce themselves. They are sexually embodied. They carry out sexual (not asexual) reproduction. And they have devised an institution to bridge the sexual divide, facilitate group living, and carry out reproduction. All human societies have this institution. They call it "marriage."[2]

But if marriage is everywhere necessary, it is also everywhere costly and fragile. People therefore tend to require social pressures to get and stay married: a strong marriage culture. In the words of University of Pennsylvania law professor Amy Wax, such a culture creates and sustains "simple rules for simple people."[3] It provides settled patterns of thought and action—a *script*—to guide people's choices toward their own long-term interest and the common good of all.

This is especially important in realms of life where our most powerful motivations do not naturally serve our true good. As the late eminent sociologist James Q. Wilson wrote, "Marriage is a socially arranged solution for the problem of getting people to stay together and care for children that the mere desire for children, and the sex that makes children possible, does not solve."[4] While personal problems give rise to personal solutions, marriage—like any social institution—addresses needs that can only be resolved socially. The universal social need presented by relationships that can produce new, dependent human beings explains why every society in the history of our race has regulated men and women's sexual relationships: has recognized marriage.

To be sure, civic associations should bear most of the burden (or, as we think, the honor) of upholding marriage culture.

Churches, synagogues, mosques, and temples, schools and recreation leagues, Boy Scouts and Camp Fire, and countless other
voluntary associations form each generation's habits of mind
and heart for marriage (and much else). Nevertheless, the state
should lend a supporting hand. By regulating marriage entry
and exit, and by helping and sometimes requiring the government as well as individuals and civic institutions to treat certain
couples as a unit, marriage law sends a strong public message
about what it takes to make a marriage—what marriage *is*. This
in turn affects people's beliefs, and therefore their expectations
and choices, about their own prospective or actual marriages.
The mutual influence of law and culture is confirmed by empirical evidence on the effects of no-fault divorce laws.[5] But if
easing the legal obstacles to divorce has had an effect, surely
removing even the hassle and stigma of a legal divorce would.
The state's influence on marriage is extensive.

Indeed, it cannot be otherwise. Abolishing civil marriage
is practically impossible. Strike the word "marriage" from the
law, and the state will still license, and attach duties and benefits to, certain bonds. Abolish these forward-looking forms of
regulation, and they will only be replaced by messier, retroac-
tive regulation—of disputes over property, custody, visitation,
and child support. What the state once did by efficient legal
presumptions, it will then do by burdensome case-by-case as-
signments of parental (especially paternal) responsibilities.[6]

The state will only discharge these tasks more or less effi-
ciently—that is, less or more intrusively. It can't escape them.
Why not? Because the *public* functions of marriage—both to
require and to empower parents (especially fathers) to care for
their children and each other—require society-wide coordination. It is not enough if, say, a particular religion presumes a
man's paternity of his wife's children, or recognizes his rights
and duties toward their mother; or if the man and his wife contract to carry out certain tasks. For private institutions can bind
only their own; private contracts bind only those who are party

to them. A major function of marriage law is to bind *all third parties* (schools, adoption agencies, summer camps, hospitals; friends, relatives, and strangers) presumptively to treat a man as father of his wife's children, husbands and wives as entitled to certain privileges and sexually off-limits, and so on. This only the state can do with any consistency.

But more than inevitable or necessary, it is *fitting* that the state should do this. Consider a comparison. Why don't even the strictest libertarians decry traffic laws? First, orderly traffic protects health and promotes efficiency, two great goods. Second, these goods are *common* in two senses: private efforts cannot adequately secure them, and yet failure to secure them has very public consequences. It is not as if we would have had the same (or even just *slightly less*) safety and efficiency of travel if people just did as they pleased, some stopping only at red lights and others only at green. Nor would damage from the resulting accidents (and slower shipments, etc.) be limited to those responsible for causing it. To ensure safe and efficient travel at all, and to limit harm to third parties, we need legal coordination. Indeed, it is no stretch to say that the state *owes* its citizens to keep minimum security and order: to these we have a *right*. Finally, unlike private associations, the state *can* secure these goods, without intolerable side effects. All this makes it appropriate for the state to set our traffic laws.

In an essay solely on political theory we might argue the details, but here we can extract from this example a widely acceptable rule: If something would serve an important good, if people have a right to it, if private groups cannot secure it well, everyone suffers if it is lost, and the state *can* secure it without undue cost, then the state may step in—and should.

All these conditions are met in the case of marriage. Marriage is not just about private problems and rewards, for which private solutions are enough. At stake are *rights*, and costs and benefits (externalities) for all society. Rights, because wherever reasonably possible, parents are entitled to bring up their own children—and children have a right to their own two parents' care, as affirmed by the United Nations Convention on the Rights of the Child.[7] And externalities are in play because failed marriages burden innocent bystanders, including children and ultimately all society. As we have seen, not only is it impossible for private groups to secure well the interests at stake but it is also many times more effective, less intrusive, and less costly for the state to do so by reinforcing marital norms than by picking up the pieces from a shattered marriage culture. Finally, promoting conjugal marriage need not and should not involve prohibiting any consensual relationship. For all these reasons, libertarians should *favor* the regulation of marriage—which is, again, practically inevitable anyway.

Let us take a closer look at the social benefits. Common sense and reliable evidence both attest to the facts that marriage benefits children, benefits spouses, helps create wealth, helps the poor especially, and checks state power.

First, as we have seen by reflection that procreation uniquely extends and perfects marriage (see chapter 2), so the best available social science suggests that children tend to do best when reared by their married mother and father. Studies that control for other factors, including poverty and even genetics, suggest that children reared in intact homes do best on the following indices:[8]

Educational achievement: literacy and graduation rates
Emotional health: rates of anxiety, depression, substance
    abuse, and suicide
Familial and sexual development: strong sense of
    identity, timing of onset of puberty, rates of teen and
    out-of-wedlock pregnancy, and rates of sexual abuse
Child and adult behavior: rates of aggression, attention
    deficit disorder, delinquency, and incarceration

Consider the conclusions of the left-leaning research institution Child Trends:

> [R]esearch clearly demonstrates that family structure matters for children, and the family structure that helps children the most is a family headed by two biological parents in a low-conflict marriage. Children in single-parent families, children born to unmarried mothers, and children in stepfamilies or cohabiting relationships face higher risks of poor outcomes. . . . There is thus value for children in promoting strong, stable marriages between biological parents. . . . [I]t is not simply the presence of two parents, . . . but the presence of *two biological parents* that seems to support children's development.[9]

According to another study, in the *Journal of Marriage and Family*, "[t]he advantage of marriage appears to exist primarily when the child is the biological offspring of both parents."[10] Recent literature reviews conducted by the Brookings Institution, the Woodrow Wilson School of Public and International Affairs at Princeton University, the Center for Law and Social Policy, and the Institute for American Values corroborate the importance of intact households for children.*[11]

Single-motherhood, cohabitation, joint custody after divorce, and stepparenting have all been reliably studied, and the result is clear: Children tend to fare worse under every one of

---

*Note that for a relationship to be ordered to procreation in this principled and empirically manifested way, sexual orientation is not a disqualifier. The union of a husband and wife bears this connection to children even if, say, the husband is also attracted to men. What is necessary is rather sexual complementarity—which two men lack even if they are attracted only to women. It is not individuals who are singled out—as being less capable of affectionate and responsible parenting, or anything else. What are instead favored as bearing a special and valuable link to childrearing are certain arrangements and the acts that complete or embody them—to which, to be sure, individuals are more or less inclined.

these alternatives to married biological parenting.[12] To make marriages more stable is to give more children the best chance to become upright and productive members of society. Note the importance of the link between marriage and children in both stages of our argument: just as it provides a powerful reason to hold the conjugal view of marriage, so it provides the central reason to make marriage a matter of public concern.

But this link is no idiosyncrasy of our view. It is amply confirmed in our law. Long before same-sex civil marriages were envisioned, courts declared that marriage "is the foundation of the family and of society, without which there would be neither civilization nor progress."[13] They recalled that "virtually every Supreme court case recognizing as fundamental the right to marry indicates as the basis for the conclusion the institution's inextricable link to procreation."[14] In their account, not just ours, "the first purpose of matrimony, by the laws of nature and society, is procreation";[15] "the procreation of children under the shield and sanction of the law" is one of the "two principal ends of marriage."[16] In fact, "marriage exists as a protected legal institution primarily because of societal values associated with the propagation of the human race."[17] Examples can be multiplied ad nauseam.[18]

A second public benefit of marriage is that it tends to help spouses financially, emotionally, physically, and socially. As the late University of Virginia sociologist Steven Nock showed, it is not that people who are better off are most likely to marry, but that marriage makes people better off. More than signal maturity, marriage can promote it. Thus men, after their wedding, tend to spend more time at work, less time at bars, more time at religious gatherings, less time in jail, and more time with family.[19]

The shape of marriage as a permanent and exclusive union ordered to family life helps explain these benefits. Permanently committed to a relationship whose norms are shaped by its aptness for family life, husbands and wives gain emotional insurance against life's temporary setbacks. Exclusively committed, they leave the sexual marketplace and thus escape its heightened risks. Dedicated to their children and each other, they enjoy the benefits of a sharpened sense of purpose. More vigorously sowing in work, they reap more abundantly its fruits. So the state's interest in productivity and social order creates an interest in marriage.[20]

Third, these two benefits of marriage—child and spousal well-being—support the conclusion of a study led by Professor W. Bradford Wilcox as part of the University of Virginia's National Marriage Project: "The core message . . . is that the wealth of nations depends in no small part on the health of the family."[21] The same study suggests that marriage and fertility trends "play an underappreciated and important role in fostering long-term economic growth, the viability of the welfare state, the size and quality of the workforce, and the health of large sectors of the modern economy."[22] These are legitimate state interests if anything is; so too, then, is marriage.

Fourth, given its economic benefits, it is no surprise that the decline of marriage most hurts the least well-off. As Kay Hymowitz argues in *Marriage and Caste in America*, the decline of the marriage culture has hurt lower-income communities and African Americans the most.[23] In fact, a leading indicator of whether someone will know poverty or prosperity is whether she knew growing up the love and security of her married mother and father.

Finally, since a strong marriage culture is good for children, spouses, indeed our whole economy, and especially the poor, it also serves the cause of limited government. Most obviously, where marriages never form or easily break down, the state expands to fill the domestic vacuum by lawsuits to determine paternity, visitation rights, child support, and alimony.

But the less immediate effects are even more extensive. As absentee fathers and out-of-wedlock births become common, a train of social pathologies follows, and with it greater demand for policing and state-provided social services. Sociologists David Popenoe and Alan Wolfe's research on Scandinavian countries shows that as marriage culture declines, the size and scope of state power and spending grow.[24]

In fact, a study by the Left-leaning Brookings Institution finds that $229 billion in welfare expenditures between 1970 and 1996 can be attributed to the breakdown of the marriage culture and the resulting exacerbation of social ills: teen pregnancy, poverty, crime, drug abuse, and health problems.[25] A 2008 study found that divorce and unwed childbearing cost taxpayers $112 billion each year.[26] And Utah State University scholar David Schramm has estimated that divorce alone costs local, state, and federal government $33 billion each year.[27]

Thus, although some libertarians would give marriage no more legal status than we give baptisms and bar mitzvahs,[28] privatizing marriage would be a catastrophe for limited government. Almost every human interest that might justify state action—health, security, educational development, social order—would also justify legally regulating marriage. A state that will not support marriage is like a doctor who will not encourage a healthy diet and exercise. Each passes over what is basic and paramount in a misplaced zeal for supplements and remedies.

IS MARRIAGE ENDLESSLY MALLEABLE?

We can now address the arguments of those on the Left who think marriage malleable to no end (call them "constructivists").[29] Marriage is for them whatever we decide to make it. There are no criteria that your relationship must meet to be a marriage—to realize the value specific to marriage as a human good. There is only the vast and gradual spectrum of more and less affectionate relations, plus our (and every) society's peculiar habit of carving out an arbitrary region on the far end of that spectrum for special social and legal treatment.[30] Hence there is no "right answer" for the state's marriage policy, any more than for the national bird: different proposals are just more or less preferable.[31]

Constructivism faces several problems, as we will show. First, it is often motivated by the fallacy, easy to dispel, that because social practices are *partly* constructed, they must be *entirely* constructed. Second, it can make no sense of major philosophical and legal traditions. Third, it also contradicts the spirit of common revisionist arguments, and would imply that many revisionists' views are, by their own lights, as radically unjust as they consider ours to be. Finally, even if constructivism were true, it would provide no good basis for the revisionist view.

Can a Social Practice Have Necessary Features?

For Professor Andrew Koppelman of Northwestern, our claim that a social practice like marriage could have necessary features that we did not choose to give it is "barely comprehensible."[32] Could *chess*, for example, have features that cannot be traced to sheer choice or custom? Why marriage, then?

For all its excellences, everything about chess is conventional. But marriage is a basic aspect of human well-being—valuable for people in itself, without our deciding to make it so, and in a way that other goods cannot substitute for.[33]

So when we say that, for example, permanent commitment is a necessary feature of marriage, we just mean that there is a distinctive human good that you can fully realize only through a vow of permanence (among other things). This is compatible with the obvious fact that many other features of marriage— like its legal benefits—vary widely across cultures and even couples. Moreover, to agree that goods have some objective features in this sense, one need not believe in God, just in some constants of *human nature*—at least across some time span.

Consider, by analogy, friendship. It clearly takes different forms across history, but no one is fooled by this into thinking that it does not retain an objective core, fixed by our social nature. True friendship requires mutual and mutually acknowledged good will and cooperation. Lacking that, a relationship between two people simply lacks the distinctive value of friendship; they owe each other none of the special consideration that friends do.

Thus also for marriage. The average 1990s American marriage and its 1890s counterpart surely have different emotional profiles, divisions of labor, and economic purposes and implications. Largely rejected in the West today, polygamy and arranged marriage have existed in many cultures. A British royal wedding looks very different from a Navajo wedding (and indeed, from a nonroyal British wedding, though not from certain New York weddings).

But none of this should unsettle proponents of the conjugal view. None of it disproves what reflection reveals: Marriage has an objective core, fixed by our nature as embodied, sexually reproductive (hence complementary) beings; and to deviate from it is to miss a crucial part of this basic human good.

First, some cross-cultural differences in marriage practice do not go to its objective core. Parties to arranged marriages, for example, may still consent to whomever they are assigned, as required for true marriage. The conjugal view neither forbids nor requires any presumption of intense feeling, or a certain economic purpose to marriage.

Second, the conjugal view is not even disproven by cultures that omit what it sees as central. No moral truth of much specificity has enjoyed universal assent—not the wrong of seeking innocent blood, nor the value of freedom from slavery, nor anything else. That makes them no less *true*.

It is natural rather to think that the most *basic* ethical principles would be most widely held; while those *derived* from more basic principles would meet with patchier understanding and assent, since we reach them by applying other principles. From this angle, the historical record is unsurprising, given the truth of the conjugal view. What it considers most basic to marriage—like bodily union and connection to family life—are nearly universal in marriage practice. And what it and our argument treat as *grounded in* these basics—permanent, exclusive commitment—is less represented. Hence the presence of polygamy in many cultures, contrasted with the nearly perfect human consensus on sexual complementarity in marriage.*

Philosophical and Legal Traditions

It might seem audacious of us to suggest that our view of the essential core of marriage is available to reasoned reflection. If so, we are just the latest in a line of audacious persons, a line that stretches back through millennia. The view that we propose has been developing for as long as there has been sustained reflection on marriage. Important philosophical and legal traditions have long distinguished friendships of all kinds from those special relationships that extend two people's union along the bodily dimension of their being and that are uniquely apt for, and enriched by, reproduction and childrearing. The three great philosophers of antiquity—Socrates, Plato, and Aristotle —as well as Xenophanes and Stoics such as Musonius Rufus defended this view—in some cases, amid highly homoerotic cultures. Especially clear is Plutarch's statement in *Erotikos* of marriage as a special kind of friendship uniquely embodied in coitus (which he, too, calls a "renewal" of marriage). He also expressly affirms in his *Life of Solon* that intercourse with an infertile spouse realizes the good of marriage—something that these other ancient thinkers took for granted, even as they (like Plutarch) denied that other sexual acts could do the same.[34]

For hundreds of years at common law, moreover, while infertility was no ground for declaring a marriage void, only coitus was recognized as consummating (completing) a marriage. No other sexual act between man and woman could. What could make sense of these two practices?

---

*Unlike a union that involves coitus, children, and permanent commitment but not (say) exclusivity, the partnerships of two men or three women lacks even what is most basic to marriage. So such partnerships cannot even be seen as imperfect participations in the good of marriage; they are not true marriages at all.

If marriage were regarded as *merely* a legal tool for keeping parents together for their children, clear evidence of infertility (like old age) would have been a ground for legally voiding a marriage. Or if the law were just targeting homosexual relationships for exclusion, it would have counted *any* sexual act between a man and woman as adequate to consummate a marriage. (To press the point, how could animus against men attracted to men have motivated the legal norm that fellatio between a man and a woman could not consummate a marriage, and indeed that a man's impotence was a ground for annulment?) Only one explanation will do: The law reflected the rational judgment that unions consummated by coitus were valuable in themselves, and different in kind from other bonds. In short, the conjugal view.

In a reply to us, Koppelman tries to explain away these legal practices by the need for bright policy lines to prevent conception out of wedlock.[35] But the wedding vow itself, a public act easier to verify without invasive questioning and harder to falsify, would have been a much "brighter" line. Anyway, the need for bright policy lines to prevent illegitimacy does nothing to explain the 2,400-year *philosophical* tradition that has likewise distinguished those uniquely comprehensive unions consummated by coitus from all others.

Constructivism and Revisionism

If marriage were merely a construct designed to achieve certain social goals, or if it differed only by degree from other bonds, then the legal and philosophical traditions we have described would be baffling. But, strikingly, so would the arguments of most *revisionists*.

First, if marriage were a fiction designed to promote social utility, there would be no natural *right* to marriage that marriage laws might violate by being defective. As long as you provided good reasons to think that your preferred marriage policy would create a larger net social benefit than any feasible alternative, there could be no justice-based argument against it. For the consistent constructivist, questions of justice should be secondary at best. And second, conversely, if constructivism were true, it would be unjust *not* to recognize polyamorous unions unless there were clear and heavy social costs to including them. But both these results are repugnant to most revisionists, and regularly contradicted by their arguments and rhetoric.

As to the first point, if (as we will show in chapter 4) abolishing the conjugal view of marriage would undermine the stability that makes marriage good for children—and thus useful to the state—then traditional marriage law *would* promise great social utility. This is only reinforced by the fact that (as we will show in chapter 6) other people's domestic needs could be met in ways that did not undermine the social benefits of traditional marriage law.

As to the second point, it is hard to see how revisionists could by their own principles resist the conclusion that justice requires recognizing polyamorous unions. (In fact, revisionist opinion-leaders, as we will show below, are increasingly endorsing such recognition.)

After all, the social costs of recognizing polyamorous relationships might include, say, increased administrative burdens for the state.* But the benefits would presumably include spousal privileges like inheritance and hospital visitation rights, and in general more practical assistance to, and social acceptance of, the relationships that Americans in an estimated 500,000 polyamorous households find most personally desirable.[36] The stigma against such people and their children would be weaker. They would feel less pressure to hide their romantic inclinations and lifestyle choices. Their economic situation could improve.

For many of them, settling for a monogamous relationship, which would lack the variety and other qualitative features specific to polyamory, might well be as unsatisfactory as settling

---

*Polygyny—whereby a man can have more than one legal wife—would undermine women's social and political equality. But the proposal considered here is *polyamory*: legal recognition of a group (of *whatever* gender distribution) as a sexual-romantic unit.

for partners to whom they are not attracted. (Nationally syndicated sex-advice columnist and same-sex civil-marriage advocate Dan Savage, for example, argues that some need multiple sexual partners in just the way that others need lovers of both sexes.[37]) The suggestion that they settle for the legal freedom to live as they choose, but without social approval, might seem offensive. Yet many rank-and-file revisionists continue to support monogamy as a legal norm.

These points therefore suggest that most people on *both* sides of our current debate reject constructivism. They agree that marriage has certain necessary features. They only disagree on whether sexual complementarity is one.

ɔ   ɔ   ɔ

The firm links between stable marriage and children's welfare, and between children's welfare and every dimension of the common good, give the state strong reasons to recognize marriage, libertarian qualms notwithstanding. But more liberal critics are also mistaken to think of marriage as *merely* an artifact of our law and culture. It is a human good with a fixed core that we are equally wise to recognize and unable to reshape.

♋ 4 ♋

What's the Harm?

HAVING COMPARED THE CONJUGAL AND REVISIONIST views of marriage and seen the benefits of recognizing marriage at all, some simply ask, *What's the harm?* Their appeal to practicality runs something like this:

> Suppose your view is coherent and even superior to the alternative as an account of the good of marriage. So what? Why not let a few thousand same-sex partners get a certificate and a certain legal status? No one would actually be worse off. *How would gay civil marriage affect your lives, liberties, or opportunities, or your own marriages?*[1]

We said in the Introduction that this debate is not about homosexuality, but about marriage. Accordingly, in chapter 6, we will show how the conjugal view respects same-sex-attracted people's equal dignity and basic needs. Here we show how the revisionist proposal would harm the institution of marriage and much else besides.

Our argument depends on three simple ideas:

1. Law tends to shape beliefs.
2. Beliefs shape behavior.
3. Beliefs and behavior affect human interests and human well-being.

Taking these truths for granted,[2] we argue that an unsound law of marriage will breed mistaken views—not just of marriage, but of parenting, common moral and religious beliefs, even friendship—that will harm the human interests affected by each of these.

WEAKENING MARRIAGE: MAKING IT HARDER TO REALIZE

No one acts in a void. We all take cues from cultural norms, shaped by the law. For the law affects our ideas of what is reasonable and appropriate. It does so by what it prohibits—you might think less of drinking if it were banned, or more of marijuana use if it were allowed—but also by what it approves. State subsidies for heavy metal promote a different view of musical merit than state sponsorship of chamber music. A school board curriculum of quack science and chauvinistic history will impart a different message about knowledge than one with more rigorous standards.

Of this point, revisionists hardly need convincing. They find civil unions insufficient even when these offer same-sex unions all the legal benefits of marriage. There is only one way to explain this: Revisionists agree that it matters what California or the United States *calls* a marriage, because this affects how Californians or Americans come to *think* of marriage.

Prominent Oxford philosopher Joseph Raz, no friend of the conjugal view, agrees:

[O]ne thing can be said with certainty [about recent changes in marriage law]. They will not be confined to adding new options to the familiar heterosexual monogamous family. They will change the character of that family. If these changes take root in our culture then the familiar marriage relations will disappear. They will not disappear suddenly. Rather they will be transformed into a somewhat different social form, which responds to the fact that it is one of several forms of bonding, and that bonding itself is much more easily and commonly dissoluble. All these factors are already working their way into the constitutive conventions which determine what is appropriate and expected within a conventional marriage and transforming its significance.[3]

Redefining civil marriage would change its meaning for everyone. Legally wedded opposite-sex unions would increasingly be defined by what they had in common with same-sex relationships.

This wouldn't just shift opinion polls and tax burdens. Marriage, the human good, would be harder to achieve. For you can realize marriage only by choosing it, for which you need at least a rough, intuitive idea of what it really is. By warping people's view of marriage, revisionist policy would make them less able to realize this basic way of thriving—much as a man confused about what friendship requires will have trouble being a friend.[4] People forming what the state called "marriage" would increasingly be forming bonds that merely resembled the real thing in certain ways, as a contractual relationship might resemble a friendship. The revisionist view would distort their priorities, actions, and motivations, to the harm of true marriage.* But it's wrong—and counterproductive—to obscure basic goods as a means to social ends (see chapter 6, dignitary harm).

---

*The revisionist proposal would teach that marriage is most centrally about emotional union. But emotional union cannot stand on its own. People really unite by *sharing a good*, but feelings are inherently private realities, which can be simultaneous but not really shared. People unite by consent, but feelings cannot be central to a vow, for we have no direct control over them.

Obscuring the good of marriage to make it harder to live out is thus the first harm of redefinition: other harms are the *effects* of misunderstanding, and failing to live out, true marriage.

WEAKENING MARRIAGE AND EXPANDING GOVERNMENT: ERODING MARITAL NORMS

Redefining marriage will also harm the material interests of couples and children. As more people absorb the new law's lesson that marriage is fundamentally about emotions, marriages will increasingly take on emotion's tyrannical inconstancy.[5] Because there is no *reason* that emotional unions—any more than the emotions that define them, or friendships generally—should be permanent or limited to two, these norms of marriage would make less sense. People would thus feel less bound to live by

---

In other words, what the revisionist proposal would obscure—and make it harder for us to live by—is the fact that marriage is first a matter of will and action: two people's consent to cooperate in ways specific to marital love, especially in bodily union of the sort made possible by sexual-reproductive complementarity, and the domestic sharing of family life to which it tends. Urgent desire and ecstatic delight, while often important motivations, are a valuable *bloom* on marriage: indicative of health and appealing in themselves, but seasonal at best. Spouses are not any less married after fifty years than on day five—or after a long day on the job than on a libidinous Saturday morning.

With the revisionist's inversion of priorities, singles deciding whom to marry might rely more on elusive emotional signals of compatibility than more prosaic indicators of fitness for marriage, such as fitness for parenting. Once married, they might increasingly carry out marital actions—sex, household cooperation, and so on—for the sake of maintaining individual (if reciprocal) satisfactions. But if chosen for the wrong reasons, even such marriage-like actions won't really build up true marriage—any more than giving a "gift" for personal gain builds up genuine friendship.

Finally, such nonmarital *motivations* might eventually change *actions*. Spouses might treat family life—which uniquely extends marriage—as less central: perhaps helpful, but perhaps a hindrance to the emotional union now treated as what marriage is really all about. And they might make their commitment more conditional on romantic attachment, impairing marital union from the utterance of "I do." These shifts would be harmful not just for their effects on social order. They would be bad in themselves, for they would impede couples from living out and building up something good in itself: true marriage.

them whenever they simply preferred to live otherwise. And, being less able to understand the value of marriage itself as a certain sort of union, even apart from its emotional satisfactions, they would miss the reasons they had for marrying or staying with a spouse as feelings waned, or waxed for others.[6]

It might seem far-fetched to predict that two values as cherished as permanence and exclusivity would wane. But we all value them so strongly in part because our culture has long embraced an ethic that supports them. As this ethic and related sentiments fade, so will support for these norms as objective standards rather than optional preferences.

As we document below, even leading revisionists now argue that if sexual complementarity is optional, so are permanence and exclusivity. This is not because the slope from same-sex unions to expressly temporary[7] and polyamorous ones is slippery, but because most revisionist arguments level the ground between them: If marriage is primarily about emotional union, why privilege two-person unions, or permanently committed ones? What is it about *emotional union*, valuable as it can be, that requires these limits?

As these norms weaken, so will the emotional and material security that marriage gives spouses. Because children fare best on most indicators of health and well-being when reared by their wedded biological parents, the same erosion of marital norms would adversely affect children's health, education, and general formation. The poorest and most vulnerable among us would likely be hit the hardest. And the state would balloon: to adjudicate breakup and custody issues, to meet the needs of spouses and children affected by divorce, and to contain and feebly correct the challenges these children face (see chapter 3).

Of course, marriage policy could go bad—and already has—in many ways, especially by the introduction of no-fault divorce laws, which make marriage contracts easier to break than contracts of any other sort. Many prominent opponents of the revisionist view—for example, Maggie Gallagher, David Blankenhorn, the U.S. Catholic bishops—also opposed other legal changes that harmed conjugal marriage.[8] For that matter, we oppose no-fault divorce laws. We are focusing here on the issue of same-sex civil marriage not because it alone matters, but because it is the focus of a live debate whose results have important consequences. Underlying people's adherence to the marital norms already in decline, after all, are the deep (if implicit) connections in their minds between marriage, bodily union, and children. Redefining marriage as revisionists propose would not just wear down but sever these ties, making it immeasurably harder to reverse other damaging recent trends and restore the social benefits of a healthy marriage culture.

MAKING MOTHER OR FATHER SUPERFLUOUS

Conjugal marriage laws reinforce the idea that the union of husband and wife is, on the whole, the most appropriate environment for rearing children—an ideal supported by the best available social science.* Recognizing same-sex relationships as marriages would legally abolish that ideal. No civil institution would reinforce the notion that men and women typically have different strengths as parents; that boys and girls tend to benefit from fathers and mothers in different ways.

To the extent that some continued to see marriage as apt for family life, they would come to think—indeed, our law, public schools, and media would teach them, and variously penalize them for denying—that it matters not, even as a rule, whether children are reared by both their mother and their father, or by a parent of each sex at all. But as the connection between marriage and parenting is obscured, as we think it would be eventually, *no* arrangement would be proposed as ideal.

And here is the central problem with either result: it would diminish the social pressures and incentives for husbands to

---

*The need for adoption (and its immense value) where the ideal is practically impossible is no argument for redefining civil marriage, a unified structure of incentives meant precisely to *reinforce* the ideal—to minimize the need for alternative, case-by-case provisions.

remain with their wives and children, or for men and women having children to marry first. Yet the resulting arrangements—parenting by divorced or single parents, or cohabiting couples—are demonstrably worse for children, as we have seen in chapter 3. So even if it turned out that studies showed no differences between same- and opposite-sex parenting, redefining marriage would undermine marital stability in ways that we know do hurt children.

That said, in addition to the data on child outcomes summarized in chapter 3, there is significant evidence that mothers and fathers have different parenting strengths—that their respective absences impede child development in different ways. Girls, for example, are likelier to suffer sexual abuse and to have children as teenagers and out of wedlock if they do not grow up with their father.[9] For their part, boys reared without their father tend to have much higher rates of aggression, delinquency, and incarceration.[10] As Rutgers University sociologist David Popenoe concludes, "The burden of social science evidence supports the idea that gender differentiated parenting is important for human development and that the contribution of fathers to childrearing is unique and irreplaceable."[11] He continues: "[W]e should disavow the notion that 'mommies can make good daddies,' just as we should disavow the popular notion . . . that 'daddies can make good mommies.' . . . The two sexes are different to the core, and each is necessary—culturally and biologically—for the optimal development of a human being."[12] In a summary of the relevant science, University of Virginia sociologist W. Bradford Wilcox finds much the same:

> Let me now conclude our review of the social scientific literature on sex and parenting by spelling out what should be obvious to all. The best psychological, sociological, and biological research to date now suggests that—on average—men and women bring different gifts to the parenting enterprise, that children benefit from having

parents with distinct parenting styles, and that family
breakdown poses a serious threat to children and to the
societies in which they live.[13]

Of course, the question of which arrangements our policies
should privilege is normative; it cannot be settled by the cause-
and-effect descriptions of social science alone. But that point
scarcely matters here, because it is impossible to generalize from
the available studies purporting to find no differences between
same-sex and married biological parenting outcomes.

Not one study of same-sex parenting meets the standard of research to which top-quality social science aspires: large, random,
and representative samples observed longitudinally. Only one—
studying only rates of primary-school progress—is even just large
and representative.[14] Several that are most frequently cited in
the media actually compare same-sex parenting outcomes with
single-, step-, or other parenting arrangements already shown to
be suboptimal.[15] Few test for more than one or two indicators
of well-being. Most resort to "snowball sampling," in which
subjects recruit their friends and acquaintances for the study.[16]
With this technique, "those who have many interrelationships
with . . . a large number of other individuals" are strongly over-
represented.[17]

As a result, psychologist Abbie Goldberg notes, studies of
same-sex parent households have focused on "white, middle-
class persons who are relatively 'out' in the gay community
and who are living in urban areas." They have overlooked
"working-class sexual minorities, racial or ethnic sexual minorities, [and] sexual minorities who live in rural or isolated
geographical areas."[18] Yet such favorably biased samples of
same-sex parents are often compared to representative (and thus
more mixed) opposite-sex parent samples.[19] As Loren Marks ob-
serves in a literature review of all fifty-nine studies on which the
American Psychological Association relied in declaring no differences between same- and opposite-sex parenting, "The available data, which are drawn primarily from small convenience

samples, are insufficient to support a strong generalizable claim either way. . . . Such a statement would not be grounded in science. To make a generalizable claim, representative, large-sample studies are needed—many of them."[20]

By contrast, consider the findings of a recent study in this area that *was* based on a large, random, and nationally representative sample, regarding outcomes in adulthood of various family structures. Compared to children of parents at least one of whom had had a gay or lesbian relationship, those reared by their married biological parents were found to have fared better on dozens of indicators, and worse on none.[21] In a critique noting some of the study's limitations, Pennsylvania State University Professor Paul Amato maintained that the study's methodological advantages still make it "probably the best that we can hope for, at least in the near future."[22]

Furthermore, the scientific literature on child well-being and same-sex parenting includes very little, reliable or otherwise, on children reared by two men. Prominent same-sex parenting scholars Timothy Biblarz and Judith Stacey, in a 2010 literature review, admitted that they "located no studies of planned gay fathers that included child outcome measures and only one that compared gay male with lesbian or heterosexual adoptive parenting."[23]

The upshot is what revisionists William Meezan and Jonathan Rauch concede in a review of the parenting literature: "What the evidence does not provide, because of the methodological difficulties we outlined, is much knowledge about whether those studied are typical or atypical of the general population of children raised by gay and lesbian couples."[24]

Ultimately, however, we have two reasons to expect that same-sex parenting is generally less effective. First, every alternative to married biological parenting that *has* been examined in high-quality studies has consistently been shown less effective: this is true of single- and stepparenting as well as parenting by cohabiting couples.[25] As Princeton and Wisconsin sociologists Sara McLanahan and Gary Sandefur found, based on four longitudinal studies of nationally representative samples including 20,000 subjects, "Children who grow up in a household with only one biological parent are worse off, on average, than children who grow up in a household with both of their biological parents . . . regardless of whether the resident parent remarries."[26] This point reinforces the idea that the state's primary interest is in upholding marital norms *to keep biological parents together*, and not simply in promoting two-parent households. Second, again, reliable studies suggest that mothers and fathers foster—and their absences impede—child development in different ways.

In short, then: redefining civil marriage might make it more socially acceptable for fathers to leave their families, for unmarried parents to put off firmer public commitment, or for children to be created for a household without a mother or father. But whatever the cause, there will be a cost to depriving children of the love and knowledge of their married mother and father.

Finally, to state the obvious: None of these points about parenting implies that men and women in same-sex relationships have weaker devotion, or less capacity for affection. After all, it is no insult to heroic single parents to point to data showing that parenting by mother and father together is more effective. What are compared in all cases are the outcomes of various parenting combinations, not individual parents.

THREATENING MORAL AND RELIGIOUS FREEDOM

The harms of redefining civil marriage would extend beyond couples and their children, to anyone who holds the conjugal view.

We Americans are not patient with those we regard as enemies of equality. People whose social attitudes and views remind us of Jim Crow, Chinese exclusion laws, and disenfranchised women experience none of the social tolerance and civility that most of us are happy to extend across vast moral and political gulfs. They are polite society's exiles, barred from the public square and even respectable jobs. The First Amendment keeps us from jailing them, but not from revoking certain civil privileges or bringing civil claims against them for living by their views.[27]

The revisionist view depends on the idea that there are no important differences between same- and opposite-sex relationships. By endorsing it, the state would imply that the conjugal view makes *arbitrary* distinctions. Conjugal marriage supporters would become, in the state's eyes, champions of invidious discrimination. This idea would lead to violations of the rights of conscience and religious freedom, and of parents' rights to direct their children's education.

The First Amendment might well keep clergy from being forced to celebrate same-sex weddings, but their lay coreligionists will not enjoy similar protections, nor will their educational and social-service institutions long escape discrimination in licensing and government contracting. From the wedding on through the honeymoon and into common life, couples transact *as a couple* with countless people. Photographers, caterers, innkeepers, adoption agency officials, parochial school administrators, counselors, foster-care and adoption providers, and others will be forced to comply with the revisionist view or lose their jobs.

We are not scaremongering: we are taking revisionists at their word. If support for conjugal marriage really is like racism, we need only ask how civil society treats racists. We marginalize and stigmatize them. Thus, in a rare departure from professional norms, a prominent law firm in April 2011 reneged on its commitment to defend the Defense of Marriage Act for the House of Representatives. In Canada, Damian Goddard was fired from his job as a sportscaster for expressing on Twitter support for conjugal marriage.[28] A Georgia counselor contracted by the Centers for Disease Control was fired after an investigation into her religiously motivated decision to refer someone in a same-sex relationship to another counselor.[29] A ministry in New Jersey lost its tax-exempt status for denying a lesbian couple use of its facility for a same-sex wedding.[30] A photographer was prosecuted by the New Mexico Human Rights Commission for declining to photograph a same-sex commitment ceremony.[31]

The courts are already eroding freedoms in this area, as champions of the rights of conscience have shown.[32] In Massachusetts, Catholic Charities was forced to give up its adoption services rather than violate its principles by placing children with same-sex cohabitants.[33] When public schools began teaching students about same-sex civil marriage, precisely on the ground that it was now the law of the commonwealth, a Court of Appeals ruled that parents had no right to exempt their students.[34] The Becket Fund for Religious Liberty reports that over "350 separate state anti-discrimination provisions would likely be triggered by recognition of same-sex marriage."[35]

Because of the mutual influence of law and culture, moreover, emerging legal trends are mirrored by social ones. The dismissal of the conjugal view as bigotry has become so deeply entrenched among revisionists that a *Washington Post* story drew denunciations and cries of journalistic bias for even implying that one conjugal view advocate was "sane" and "thoughtful."[36] Outraged readers compared the profile to a hypothetical puff piece on a Ku Klux Klan member.[37] A *New York Times* columnist has called conjugal marriage proponents (including one of us by name) "bigots."[38] Organizations pushing the legal redefinition of marriage label themselves as champions of "human rights" and opponents of "hate."[39]

We agree, of course, that it is within the state's due powers to restrict invidious discrimination—racist, sexist, or otherwise—and that society may marginalize noxious views by marginalizing their champions. But it had better be right that these views are false and harmful. If they are not noxious but suppressed anyway, then it is society that hurts the common good, by curbing freedoms of speech, religion, and conscience for nothing more than ideological uniformity.

UNDERMINING FRIENDSHIP

We often hear arguments for and against the idea that redefinition would weaken marriage and threaten religious freedom. But it is a point lost on both sides of this debate that the social prevalence of the revisionist view would make things harder on single people: As marriage is defined simply as the most valuable or only kind of deep communion, it becomes harder to find emotional and spiritual intimacy in nonmarital friendships.

Consider in this connection *Atlantic* blogger Ta-Nehisi Coates's admission that he had until recently never considered the possibility of deep nonromantic friendship. Reading about historical examples of it "actually opened up some portion of my own imagination—the possibility of feeling passionate, but not sexual, about someone who I wasn't related to," he confessed. " 'Passion' isn't a word that often enters into the description [of] friendships these days. And yet [it's] present in the writings of previous generations"—when people recognized marriage as the paradigm of one *type* of intimacy among others, and did not simply *equate* intimacy with marriage.

But the revisionist view tends to do just that. Revisionists cannot define marriage in terms of real bodily union or family life, so they tend to define it instead by its *degree* or *intensity*. Marriage is *simply* your closest relationship, offering *the most* of the one basic currency of intimacy: shared emotion and experience. As a federal judge recently put it in a case striking down California's conjugal marriage law, " 'marriage' is the name that society gives to the relationship that matters most between two adults."[40]

The more we absorb this assumption, the less we value deep friendship in its own right. Self-disclosure, unembarrassed reliance, self-forgetfulness, extravagant expressions of affection, and other features of companionship come to seem gauche—or even feel like unwelcome impositions—outside romance and marriage.[41] We come to see friendships as mere rest stops on the way back to family life. It becomes harder to share experiences with our friend that we could just as well have shared with our spouse, without seeming to detract from our marriage.

The conjugal view, by contrast, gives marriage a definite shape, as ordered to true bodily union and thus to family life. If the revisionist view sees single people as just settling for *less*, the conjugal view leaves room for different forms of communion, each with its own distinctive scale and form of companionship and support. It keeps from making marriage totalizing: it clarifies what we owe our spouses in marital love; what we owe it to them not to share with others; and what we could share now with them, now with others, without any compromise of our marriage.

The conjugal view's restoration could thus help us recover the companionate value of friendship: that bond which King David called "more wonderful to me than the love of women," which Augustine described as "two souls in one body";[42] a bond all the sweeter for being chosen, but no less demanding for those who know its depths.

THE "CONSERVATIVE" OBJECTION

We have seen that redefining civil marriage would affect how we conduct our sexual relationships, how we parent, how we treat conscientious dissent, and how we deal with our friends. Such changes in thought and action would affect people's interests—not just those of children, but of spouses, the unmarried, religious believers of various traditions, and others.

It remains for us to address a common objection to part of this argument. Some say that adopting the revisionist view, far from destabilizing the institution of marriage, would actually strengthen it, by imposing traditional marital norms—conservative values—on more relationships.

This point is usually offered as a stand-alone argument for same-sex civil marriage. But note its limits: It does not show the revisionist view of marriage to be *true* or the conjugal view false (much less inconsistent or bigoted). Untouched are our claims that fathers matter as well as mothers, and that revisionism threatens this ideal. The point does not allay concerns about moral and religious freedom, or the diminution of friendship. In fact, it does not even rebut our argument that marital norms would come to make less sense in a revisionist world.

In other words, those who make this allegedly conservative claim are suggesting only that it would be good if we used the law to reshape same-sex unions according to the traditional norms of marriage, whatever the point or likelihood of getting them to take and keep the desired shape. But even stripped to its modest core, the objection fails.

It fails because it assumes that the state can effectively encourage adherence to norms in relationships where those norms have no deep rational basis—no reason for partners to stay together and exclusive, even if desire wanders or wanes or attachment erodes. Laws that restrict people's freedom for no deep purpose are not likely to last, much less to influence behavior.[43]

But redefining civil marriage would not just be idle in this respect; it would be counterproductive. Over time, people tend to abide *less* by any given norms, the less those norms make sense. To say it again, if marriage is understood as an essentially emotional union, then marital norms, especially permanence and exclusivity, will make less sense. But whatever the morality of flouting these norms in other relationships, they *do*, in opposite-sex relationships, serve the interests that hook the state into recognizing and supporting marriages in the first place.

So those who champion the conservative objection are right to think that redefining civil marriage would produce a convergence—but it would be a convergence in exactly the wrong direction. Rather than imposing traditional norms on same-sex relationships, abolishing the conjugal view would tend to erode the basis for those norms in *any* relationship.

This is not an abstract matter. If the conjugal conception of marriage were right, what would you expect the sociology of same-sex romantic unions to be like? In the absence of strong reasons to abide by marital norms, you would expect to see less regard for those norms in both practice and theory. On both counts, you would be right.

Consider the norm of monogamy. Judith Stacey—a prominent New York University professor who is in no way regarded as a fringe figure, in testifying before Congress against the Defense of Marriage Act—expressed hope that the revisionist view's triumph would give marriage "varied, creative, and adaptive contours . . . [leading some to] question the dyadic limitations of Western marriage and seek . . . small group marriages."[44] In their statement "Beyond Same-Sex Marriage," more than three hundred "LGBT and allied" scholars and advocates—including prominent Ivy League professors—call for legally recognizing sexual relationships involving more than two partners.[45] University of Calgary Professor Elizabeth Brake thinks that justice requires us to use legal recognition to "denormalize[] heterosexual monogamy as a way of life" and correct for "past discrimination against homosexuals, bisexuals, polygamists, and care networks."[46]

What about the connection to family life? Andrew Sullivan, a self-styled proponent of the conservative case for same-sex civil marriage, says that marriage has become "primarily a way in which two adults affirm their emotional commitment to one another."[47] E. J. Graff celebrates the fact that recognizing same-sex unions would change the "institution's message" so that it would "ever after stand for sexual choice, for cutting the link between sex and diapers."[48] Enacting same-sex civil marriage "does more than just fit; it announces that marriage has changed shape."[49]

And exclusivity? Mr. Sullivan, who has extolled the "spirituality" of "anonymous sex," also thinks that the "openness" of same-sex unions could enhance the bonds of husbands and wives:

> Same-sex unions often incorporate the virtues of friendship more effectively than traditional marriages; and at times, among gay male relationships, the openness of the

contract makes it more likely to survive than many heterosexual bonds. . . . [T]here is more likely to be greater
understanding of the need for extramarital outlets between two men than between a man and a woman. . . .
[S]omething of the gay relationship's necessary honesty,
its flexibility, and its equality could undoubtedly help
strengthen and inform many heterosexual bonds.[50]

"Openness" and "flexibility" here are Sullivan's euphemisms
for sexual infidelity. Similarly, in a *New York Times Magazine*
profile, same-sex civil marriage activist Dan Savage encourages
spouses to adopt "a more flexible attitude" about allowing each
other to seek sex outside their marriage. A piece in *The Advocate*, a gay-interest newsmagazine, supports our point still more
candidly:

Anti-equality right-wingers have long insisted that allowing gays to marry will destroy the sanctity of "traditional
marriage," and, of course, the logical, liberal party-line
response has long been "No, it won't." But what if—for
once—the sanctimonious crazies are right? Could the
gay male tradition of open relationships actually alter
marriage as we know it? And would that be such a bad
thing?[51]

As the article's blurb reads, "We often protest when homo-
phobes insist that same sex marriage will change marriage for
straight people too. But in some ways, they're right."[52]

Again, these are not our words, but those of leading supporters of same-sex civil marriage. If you believe in permanence and
exclusivity but would redefine civil marriage, take note.

In fact, some revisionists have embraced the goal of weaken-
ing the institution of marriage *in these very terms*. "[Former
President George W.] Bush is correct," says revisionist advocate
Victoria Brownworth, ". . . when he states that allowing same-
sex couples to marry will weaken the institution of marriage.

. . . It most certainly will do so, and that will make marriage a far better concept than it previously has been."[53] Professor Ellen Willis, another revisionist, celebrates the fact that "conferring the legitimacy of marriage on homosexual relations will introduce an implicit revolt against the institution into its very heart."[54]

Michelangelo Signorile, a prominent gay activist, urges people in same-sex relationships to "demand the right to marry not as a way of adhering to society's moral codes but rather to debunk a myth and radically alter an archaic institution."[55] They should "fight for same-sex marriage and its benefits and then, once granted, redefine the institution of marriage completely, because the most subversive action lesbians and gay men can undertake . . . is to transform the notion of 'family' entirely."[56]

And the Western world's limited experience so far suggests that these ideas play out in policy. Since countries have begun recognizing same-sex unions, officials have proposed bills, made administrative decisions, or allowed lawsuits challenging nearly every other traditional norm: Mexico City has considered expressly temporary marriage licenses.[57] A federal judge in Utah has allowed a legal challenge to anti-bigamy laws as violations of religious liberty and infringements of equality.[58] A public notary in Brazil has recognized a triad as a civil union, saying in almost so many words that the redefinition of marriage required it: "[T]he move reflected the fact that the idea of a 'family' had changed. . . . 'For better or worse, it doesn't matter, but what we considered a family before isn't necessarily what we would consider a family today.' "[59]

Some revisionists, like Jonathan Rauch, sincerely hope to preserve traditional marital norms.[60] But the prediction that they would be weakened is backed up not only by reflection on what these norms are grounded in, along with surveys of revisionist arguments, rhetoric, and the progression of their policy proposals, but also by preliminary social science.

In the 1980s, Professors David McWhirter and Andrew Mattison, themselves in a romantic relationship, set out to disprove popular beliefs about gay partners' lack of adherence to sexual exclusivity. Of those that they surveyed, whose relationships had lasted from one to thirty-seven years, more than 60 percent had begun the relationship expecting sexual exclusivity, but not one couple stayed sexually exclusive longer than five years.[61] McWhirter and Mattison concluded that, by the end, "[t]he expectation for outside sexual activity was the rule for male couples and the exception for heterosexuals."[62] Far from disproving popular beliefs, they confirmed them.

The *New York Times* more recently reported on a study finding that exclusivity was not the norm among gay partners: " 'With straight people, it's called affairs or cheating,' said Colleen Hoff, the study's principal investigator, 'but with gay people it does not have such negative connotations.' "[63]

In fact, the difference touches more than just expectations. Evidence suggests that exclusivity affects men's satisfaction in opposite-sex relationships more than in same-sex ones. According to one study, sexually "open" gay relationships last longer.[64] According to another, "no differences were found between [gay] couples who were sexually monogamous and nonmonogamous on measures of relationship satisfaction and relationship agreement."[65] By contrast, 99 percent of opposite-sex couples expect—that is, demand of each other and anticipate—sexual exclusivity in their marriage,[66] and violations of it are "the leading cause of divorce across 160 cultures and are one of the most frequent reasons that couples seek marital therapy."[67]

Some offer evolutionary explanations for these differences: in opposite-sex couples, where children regularly result, fidelity serves the interests of children by keeping their parents' attention and resources from being diverted. It represents a compromise between women's generally higher interest in sex that expresses affection (and men's interest in not investing in other men's children) on the one hand, and men's generally higher interest in sexual variety on the other.[68] Whether one embraces these explanations, or the ethical reflection on the goods at stake that we offer above, or both of these accounts as mutually reinforcing, it is easy to see how the status of exclusivity would differ for same- and opposite-sex relationships.

On the questions of numbers of partners and relationship longevity, we must avoid stereotypes, which exaggerate unfairly, but also consider social data in light of what we argue about the weaker rational *basis* for permanence and monogamy outside opposite-sex relationships. A 1990s U.K. survey of more than five thousand men found that the median numbers of partners over the previous five years for men with exclusively heterosexual inclinations was two, with bisexual inclinations was seven, and with exclusively homosexual inclinations was ten.[69] A U.S. survey found that the average number of sexual partners since the age of eighteen for men who identified as homosexual or bisexual was over two and a half times as many as the average for heterosexual men.[70] And a study of same-sex civil marriages in Norway and Sweden found that "divorce risks are higher in same-sex partnerships than opposite-sex marriages and . . . unions of lesbians are considerably less stable, or more dynamic, than unions of gay men."[71]

Finally, as we argued above, preliminary evidence suggests that even same-sex civil marriage cannot impose, by sheer social pressure, norms that make less sense as general requirements for same-sex relationships. The *New York Times* reported on a San Francisco State University study: "[G]ay nuptials are portrayed by opponents as an effort to rewrite the traditional rules of matrimony. Quietly, outside of the news media and courtroom spotlight, many gay couples are doing just that."[72]

So there is no reason to believe, and abundant reason to doubt, that redefining civil marriage would make people more likely to abide by its norms. Instead, it would further undermine people's grasp of the principled basis for those norms. Nothing more than a weak wall of sentiment would remain to hold back the tide of harmful social change.

Justice and Equality

We have argued that the revisionist view is not only internally inconsistent and at odds with widely accepted principles about marriage, but harmful to implement. Revisionists often raise similar objections to the conjugal view: that it is inconsistent in recognizing infertile marriages, and at odds with the widely accepted principle of equal access to marriage. Here we show that both objections fail. The conjugal view is internally consistent, and it respects the principle that people of all inclinations have equal dignity and title to all the same rights.

THE CASE OF INFERTILITY

Revisionists argue that proponents of the conjugal view cannot give a principled basis for recognizing infertile couples' unions that would not equally apply to same-sex unions.

This challenge is easily met. An infertile man and woman can together still form a true marriage—a comprehensive union—which would differ only in degree, not type, from a fertile union before or after the first childbirth. So recognizing such unions as marriages has none of the costs of recognizing same-sex or other unions as marriages; most of the benefits of recognizing fertile unions; and at least one *additional* benefit.

Still True Marriages

To form a true marriage, a couple needs to establish the comprehensive mind-and-body union that would be completed by and apt for procreation and domestic life and that thus inherently calls for permanent and exclusive commitment.

Every male-female couple capable of consummating their commitment can have all three features. With or without children, on the wedding night or ten years later, these relationships are all comprehensive in the three senses specific to marriage, with its distinctive sort of value. Without exception, same-sex and multiple-partner unions are not.

Of course, this would not be true of infertile couples if they could not perform marital acts. Princeton Professor Stephen Macedo and Northwestern Law Professor Andrew Koppelman argue that our view implies that they cannot.[1] What is clear is that people are composites of body and mind, so a marital act between two people must combine the right *behavior* with the right *intention*. It must be a *real bodily union* (coitus) that seals a certain kind of *union of minds and hearts*. So the question is whether infertile couples can have the correct intention and behavior for a marital act. The answer is that they can.

Take intention. For any couple's act of bodily union to be an act of *marital* union, they need not choose it for the sake of conceiving, but simply to embody, or make concrete, their marriage: their specific, marital form of love, their permanent and exclusive commitment. This means, among other things, intending to seek such bodily union only with each other (exclusivity) until death (permanence). Clearly, while (say) the intention to keep a sexually open union is an impediment here, infertility is not—unless it prevents the behavior they choose from being organic bodily union in the first place.

And it does not. An act of sexual intercourse is organic bodily union whether or not it causes conception, as our law has always recognized. The man and woman's bodies are still united in coitus much as organs of a single body are united: toward a single biological good (reproduction) of the whole that they compose together. So the spouses are indeed united bodily, and may be comprehensively. Because coitus would be fulfilled by conception, it extends their specific (marital) kind of commitment onto the plane of the sexual and bodily. Even for infertile couples, the deep symmetry between bond and act remains: both would be naturally fulfilled by children.

The nature of the spouses' behavior now—as biological coordination toward a certain end (which might or might not also be a subjective goal)—cannot depend on what happens hours later outside their control: whether a sperm penetrates an egg. Each stage of a multistage process like reproduction keeps its identity, whatever happens at later stages. This is clear in individual functions like digestion. Different parts of that process—chewing, swallowing, stomach action, nutrient absorption—are ordered to the broader goal of nourishing the organism. But your chewing and stomach action remain so ordered (remain digestive acts) even when your intestines fail to absorb nutrients, and even if you know so before you eat.[2] This is just part of what sets biological processes apart: they don't depend on our goals or beliefs.

Likewise, the behavioral part of the reproductive process (coitus) remains ordered to reproduction even when nonbehavioral factors—like low sperm count—prevent conception, and spouses expect this beforehand. So coitus remains a form of bodily coordination, or joint functioning toward a single bodily end (whether or not it is an end they seek), and thus a form of bodily union. And that—being a bodily union, not actually causing conception—is what makes coitus, if chosen with the intention to embody or renew their marriage, a valuable part of a valuable whole: a marital act that extends a marital, or comprehensive, union.

That is why, as our law has always recognized, infertility is no impediment to marriage—something good in itself, which can thus exist with its distinctive value absent children.

A friendship of two men or two women is also valuable in itself. But lacking the capacity for organic bodily union, it cannot be valuable specifically *as a marriage*: it cannot be the comprehensive union on which aptness for procreation and distinctively marital norms depend.

None of the Costs

The idea that infertile couples can form a marriage is not just abstract: it means that their unions bear on the common good much as fertile ones do.

But before considering its benefits, we note that recognizing infertile marriages has none of the *costs* of recognizing same-sex, polyamorous, or other nonmarital unions (see chapter 4). It does not make it harder for people to realize the basic good of marriage, for it does not undermine the public's grasp of the nature of true marriage. Nor does it undermine marital *norms*, which are grounded in that nature, or make fathers or mothers seem superfluous. It prejudices no one's religious or moral freedom. Also, by preserving the idea that marriage differs from other bonds by the *type* of sharing it involves (bodily union), not just the amount (the most), recognizing infertile unions does nothing to diminish friendship or make spiritual intimacy seem alien to it.

Many of the Benefits

Practically speaking, many couples believed to be infertile end up having children who would be served by their parents' healthy marriage; in any case, the effort to determine fertility would require unjust invasions of privacy. (This presumably represents common ground with revisionists, who would not, for example, inquire into a couple's level of affection before granting a marriage license, however deeply they had absorbed the view that emotional intimacy made a marriage.)

Furthermore, even an obviously infertile couple can live out the features of true marriage, and so contribute to a strong marriage culture. This makes couples who might conceive more likely to form a marriage and abide by its norms. That in turn ensures that more children are reared by their married biological parents. Death and tragedy make the gap impossible to close, and for that reason adoption is a blessing. But a healthier marriage culture would make the gap shrink.

Indeed, failing to recognize the unions of infertile couples may really violate the principle of equality to which revisionists appeal, since infertile as well as fertile couples can form unions of the same *kind*: true marriages, comprehensive unions. Absent strong reasons for it, this kind of differential treatment would be unfair.

A Special Benefit

Finally, to recognize only fertile marriages would be to suggest that marriage is valuable only as a means to children—and not what it truly is, a good in itself. So recognizing the marriages of infertile couples serves at least one purpose *better* than recognizing only fertile unions does: to recall for us the truth, crucial for healthy and stable marriages generally, that marriage has value in itself.

Thus, though the conjugal view does not restrict marriage certificates to spouses with children, its success would tend to limit children to families led by spouses, and to contribute to marital stability. So there is no easy distinction between the moral purposes of marriage law and its social utility. The more spouses (including infertile ones) reflect by their lives the truth about what marriage requires, the more saturated we will all be in those truths, so that more families *with* children will stay intact. As these truths dim, so will our prospects as a culture.

THE INJUSTICE OF BANS ON
INTERRACIAL MARRIAGE

Revisionists often equate traditional marriage laws with laws banning interracial marriage. People cannot control their sexual orientation any more than their skin color,[3] they argue, so there is no rational basis for distinguishing relationships by either: the freedom to marry the person one loves is a fundamental right.[4] The state discriminates against same-sex partners by interfering with this basic right, thus refusing them its equal protection.[5] To those who make this argument, it is nearly self-evident; they see it as decisive.

We affirm as true, indeed self-evident, that all human beings have equal moral dignity, equal basic rights under the law, and a right in justice against every invidious distinction. This principle covers men attracted to men, and women attracted to women, and for that matter men and women inclined to polyamory, as well as it does redheads, and people born on Tuesdays. But it yields no right to legal recognition of same-sex relationships (see chapter 6). The analogy to interracial marriages, in particular, fails for many reasons. At least two are truly decisive.

First, opponents of interracial marriage did not deny that marriage (understood as a union consummated by conjugal acts) was possible between blacks and whites any more than segregationists argued that some feature of the whites-only water fountains made it impossible for blacks to drink from them. The whole point of antimiscegenation laws in the United States was to prevent the genuine possibility of interracial marriage from being realized or recognized, in order to maintain white supremacy. Many states refused to recognize marriages between black slaves for similar, white supremacist, reasons; and marriages between two different nonwhite races, having no effect on white supremacy, were generally allowed.[6]

By contrast, the current debate is precisely over whether the kind of union with marriage's essential features can exist between two men or two women. Revisionists would not leave our basic understanding of marriage intact and simply expand the pool of people eligible to marry (as many states did to allow slaves to marry). They would abolish the conjugal view of marriage from our law and replace it with the revisionist view. They would make civil marriage no longer a comprehensive union but an emotional one, to which sex is of no more value than the feeling it fosters; to which procreation is no more specially related, spouses' preferences aside, than deep conversation or badminton; for which permanence and exclusivity are optional.

Second, while history compels the conclusion that hostility or animus motivated antimiscegenation laws, it *rules out* this explanation of traditional marriage laws. Yes, homosexual acts were widely condemned for centuries in the West, and still are by many people and religious traditions. *But so were (and are) analogous acts between a husband and wife.* The basics of our marriage law allowed marriages to be consummated by no act other than coitus, *even between a legally wedded man and woman.* Those basics long predate the nineteenth-century medicalization of homosexuality and the subsequent rise of gay cultural identity, let alone the Stonewall riots. Some cultures, as in ancient Greece, recognized only opposite-sex unions as marriages even as they *celebrated* homoeroticism. Only ignorance of these facts could sustain the idea that antigay animus shaped our marriage law and that of every other culture.

The analogy to antimiscegenation also goes wrong by relying on the false assumption that any distinction is unjust discrimination. Suppose that the legal incidents of marriage were made available to all committed, exclusive romantic couplings. We would still, by the love-makes-a-marriage logic of revisionists, be discriminating against those seeking open, expressly temporary, polygynous, polyandrous, or polyamorous unions. After all, people can find themselves experiencing sexual and romantic desire for multiple partners, concurrent or serial. They are free not to act on their sexual desires, but this is true of all of us.

So why not recognize open, temporary, or polyamorous unions? Revisionists might answer that people should be free to enter such relationships, but that they do not merit legal recognition. Why? Some may reply that doing so would have bad social consequences. We answered them in chapter 3. But many will join conjugal marriage supporters in replying that marriage as such *just cannot take these forms*, or can do so only immorally. Recognizing these relationships as marriages would be, depending on the case, confused or immoral.

Whoever replies in this way—and many on both sides do—must accept three principles.

First, marriage is not a legal construct with totally malleable contours—it is not "just a contract." Instead, some sexual relationships are instances of a distinctive kind of bond that has its own value and structure, which the state did not invent and has no power to redefine. As we argued in chapter 1, marriages are, like the relationship between parents and their children or between the parties to an ordinary promise, *moral realities* that create moral privileges and obligations between people with or without legal enforcement. Whatever practical realities may draw the state into recognizing marriage in the first place (e.g., children's needs), the state, once involved, must get marriage *right* to avoid obscuring the shape of this human good.

Thus, when some states forbade interracial marriage, they either attempted to keep people from forming true marriages or denied legal status to the same. And if the state conferred the same status on a man and his two closest friends (whatever their sex), this would not make them married. It would involve giving the title of civil marriage to what is, in truth, no marriage at all.

Second, the state is within its rights to recognize only true marriages. People who cannot enter marriages so understood (for whatever reasons) are not denied a right to *marriage*, even when they cannot control the factors that keep them single.

All legal recognition divides the world in two: what is recognized, and everything else. Laws that distinguish marriage from other bonds will *always* leave some arrangements out. You cannot move an inch toward showing that marriage policy violates equality, without first showing what marriage is and why it should be recognized legally at all. That will establish which criteria (like kinship status) are relevant, and which (like race) are irrelevant to marriage policy. It will establish when a marriage is what is going unrecognized, and when what is excluded is something else entirely (we revisit and develop this point in chapter 6).

Third, and finally, there is no general right to marry the person you love, if this means a right to have any consensual relationship recognized as marriage. There is only a general right not to be prevented from forming a true marriage.

There is, in short, no direct line from the principle of equality to same-sex civil marriage. Equality requires treating like cases alike. To know which count as "alike," we have to know what marriage is and how recognizing it helps society. But to these questions, the conjugal view has the superior answers: it is more consistent with our convictions about this human good (chapters 1 and 2), and better for society (chapter 4). So the argument from equality fails.

✖ 6 ✖

A Cruel Bargain?

MARRIAGE IS A COMPREHENSIVE UNION. THE STATE HAS excellent reasons to recognize it, and excellent reasons to enact the *correct* view of it. These reasons are rooted not in some obscure ideology or private interest, but variously and deeply in human nature and the common good of all society, which reason and experience lay bare. These have been our themes.

As we have pointed out, many same-sex-attracted men and women—including some in gay or lesbian relationships—agree with our conclusion.[1] Some do so because they object to casting same-sex unions in a mold designed for husbands and wives,[2] but others cite reasons identical to or much like the ones we offer.[3]

Even so, you might fear that whatever gains the conjugal view wins for the many, it wins at a cruel cost for the few. If we agreed, we would not just lament our conclusions, but retract them. No good argument starts by discounting anyone's interests, or ends in a policy that does. But the conjugal view requires no such thing.

What we might call for short "the cruelty objection"—or, in positive terms, "the argument from compassion"—is hard to condense to a few points. If addressing its concerns one-by-one seems to diminish them, this is only because, though serious, they have been swirled together in our public discourse, each gathering speed and force from the others. We isolate them here to give sustained attention to each.

Marriage is a source of great joy for most people. Most spouses rely extensively on its legally guaranteed practical benefits. Because of the social importance of marriage, marriage law can be used to reinforce a larger scheme of oppression, as it was for decades in the American South.

Accordingly, the objection considered here charges that traditional marriage law harms the personal fulfillment, the practical interests, and the social standing of same-sex-attracted people. Each of these claims has been, at some point or other, the primary public argument for same-sex civil marriage. We treat them in roughly the order in which they so reigned.

PRACTICAL NEEDS

Andrew Sullivan questions one of us:

> It also seems to me to be important to ask George what he proposes should be available to gay couples. Does he believe that we should be able to leave property to one another without other family members trumping us? That we should be allowed to visit one another in hospital? That we should be treated as next-of-kin in medical or legal or custody or property tangles? Or granted the same tax status as straight married couples? These details matter to real people living actual lives.[4]

Note that the benefits cited have nothing to do with whether a relationship is or is presumed to be sexual. Suppose the law grants these bundled benefits as civil unions to two men in a sexual partnership. Should it not also grant them to two bachelor brothers committed to sharing a home? These two bonds would differ in many ways, but which of those ways would make tax breaks or inheritance rights less fitting or useful for one? Both bonds would involve sharing household burdens, and building up that common stock of memories, sympathies, and mutual reliance that makes each the other's best proxy in emergencies, his default beneficiary in death, and the like.

What's more, to the extent that our goal is to provide same-sex romantic unions with ready access to important benefits, such a scheme would be more effective. It would be available even to same-sex partners who did not want to liken their unions to heterosexual marital unions—an assimilation that makes some same-sex partners see gay civil marriage as a "mixed blessing," if a blessing at all.[5]

Of course, a policy that granted legal benefits to any two adults upon request—romantic partners, widowed sisters, cohabiting celibate monks—would offer no rival definition of marriage, or cause the harm of policies that do (see chapter 4), for it would not limit benefits to relationships that were presumed to be sexual. To these "sex-neutral" civil unions, we have no objection in principle.[6]

People can normally secure these benefits privately, for example, through power of attorney, which we think should always be available. So before we enact sex-neutral civil unions, we should consider: What specific common good would they serve? Would this good depend on policing entry into and exit from such unions, as regulation does? Would it permit diluting the special status of civil marriage? Formalizing sex-neutral unions might be most useful where people lack the education or resources to make private arrangements. But if such a proposal survives our objections to the redefinition of civil marriage, that is because it is no actual redefinition of civil marriage.

DIGNITARY HARM

We all have more than material interests. Being equal in dignity, we should stand equal before the law and our fellow human beings. Even if same-sex partners can meet their material needs in states that have traditional marriage laws, do these laws diminish their social status by recognizing others' relationships but not theirs?

We are each related to countless people in countless ways that have no legal status, and no one thinks this an offense to social dignity. To make this objection work, we must make it specific: people are stigmatized when their *marriages* are not recognized while others' are.

The objection itself thus provides no separate argument for revisionism. It works only if that view is already shown to be correct. If, instead, some romantic couplings really are not marriages, then there is no more offense to equality in not recognizing them than there is in excluding roommates or deep conversation partners or committed romantic triads. Even the *appearance* of inequality would be only as widespread as the revisionist view. As the conjugal view prevails, the force of this concern shrinks.

Now assume, if only for a moment, the conjugal view. From this perspective, it becomes clear that, in a deep sense, the state *cannot* make two men or two women married. It can grant people living together certain legal incidents, and it can (as we think it should) allow them to make private legal arrangements. It can even treat same- and opposite-sex relationships as if they were the same in every important way; but it cannot *make* them so. So we do not deny same-sex or polyamorous partners *access to marriage* by preserving the conjugal view.*

---

*Some people wonder how something naturally occurring—and thus, some theists conclude, intended by God—could impede a good such as marriage. We do not pretend to know the genesis of same-sex attraction, but we consider it ultimately irrelevant to this debate. In this, we agree with gay advocate John Corvino, who admits that "there are plenty of genetically influenced traits that are nevertheless undesirable"—or, more modestly, that can impede a certain good. John Corvino, "Nature? Nurture? It Doesn't Matter," *Independent Gay Forum*, August 12, 2004, http://igfculturewatch.com/2004/08/12/nature-nurture-it-doesnt-matter/.

Surely the fact that something is natural in the sense that it is not *chosen* proves nothing: Prior special obligations to one's family of origin can be natural

Whatever the state says, in other words, no same-sex or group relationship will include organic bodily union, or find its inherent fulfillment in procreation, or *require*, quite apart from the partners' personal preferences, what these two features demand: permanent and exclusive commitment. Nor can sheer legislative will make these differences meaningless, or make disregarding them harmless to the common good.

Redefining civil marriage means *pretending otherwise*. But so pretending—for two men; or for a man and woman with too many duties to commit totally, or too little interest to commit sexually, or too much interest in others—would be at best a "noble lie," and at worst a paternalistic effort at shielding people from the truth about marriage. Like trying to win a just war using nationalistic textbooks (thus harming the cause of truth), such a policy would, as a means to honest goals, obscure a basic good: marriage (see the first section of chapter 4). And it would win its dubious victory for social dignity at the cost of still other public goods (see chapter 4).

But let us not dwell on the letter of this objection and miss its spirit. There is no denying the long and tragic history of cruelty toward people (especially, but by no means only, men) attracted to members of their own sex. They have known ridicule, discrimination, and worse. So a revisionist might ask: even if traditional marriage laws are not unjust, might the revisionist proposal protect certain vulnerable people against mistreatment for which there is, alas, significant historical precedent?

We are not convinced that people motivated by hatred would be moved by changes in marriage law. We think that for this purpose, the law makes a blunt instrument: revamping it has the unintended harmful effects that we have discussed; and

---

in this sense and yet impede marriage. Conversely, if we discovered (plausibly) a genetic basis for male desire for multiple partners, that would be an argument for polygamy; and if we discovered (implausibly) that no sexual desire had a genetic basis, we would not have an argument against all marriage. There is just no connection between the origin of same-sex desire and the possibility of same-sex marriage.

doing so precisely to mark which individuals are normal might further marginalize those who, for whatever reason, remain unmarried.

Yet we cannot rule out that some might—incorrectly, as we have shown—just *take* traditional marriage laws to reflect the deplorable belief that same-sex-attracted people are not entitled to equal rights, or that their interests matter less. But they would draw this harmful inference only if they thought that same-sex relationships really *were* marriages, such that society's reason for not recognizing them could only be that the partners themselves were somehow undeserving.

Thus, where conjugal marriage law prevails, one way to dissolve any notion that same-sex-attracted people matter less is precisely to promote the conjugal view: to make plain its *reasons* for requiring complementarity in marriage. The better people understood those reasons, the less they would mistakenly read into the law an endorsement of animus, which is a force to be rejected no matter whom it targets, and no matter how worthy the moral theory it highjacks for respectability.

PERSONAL FULFILLMENT, PUBLIC RECOGNITION

The most common and most passionate objection lodged today against traditional marriage laws charges them with inflicting a harm that eludes such easy labels as "material" or "social." It seems to be an emotional, psychological, even spiritual harm: a hollow in the soul that only the joys of marriage could fill. Do traditional marriage laws not deprive same-sex-attracted people in this way?

Let us specify the objection in order to answer it fully and directly.

In a highly mobile age, we want continuity. Our spouses, permanent breakfast partners, reliable sources and objects of interest and affection, anchor us. What we do alone has less verve than what we share: spouses are witnesses to our adult-

hoods; they are our living and dynamic diaries. We want know-
ing consolation and informed advice: spouses have license to
plumb our past and present and our most private ambitions.
We want the security of a first responder in emergencies, ready
counsel in our distress, de facto company in defeat, and, for
every personal victory, a two-way tie. Spouses typically provide
all these goods.

Besides, marriage itself is a school of virtue. As fear gives
way to surrender, as the exhilaration of surrender gives way
to laboriousness and then to the serenely familiar, we mature.
Stretched across another life's peaks and troughs, our ego is un-
raveled. What we want from our spouses, we learn ever more to
give. In vacations and bedside vigils, grand projects and modest
self-denials, our spouses call forth in us new excellences, somehow making us feel all the while that we are most at ease, and
most ourselves, when they are near.

Now then, the revisionist asks, shall we deny all this to thousands of men and women?

We shouldn't, and we don't. Whether or not these companionate ideals are equally healthy to seek, all in one bond, and
all specifically in marriage, the general desire that animates
them—to know and serve one who knows and serves us—is the
desire to love. No aim is nobler.

But traditional marriage law *does not deny these companionate ideals to anyone.* It does not discourage them or even
prevent people from encouraging them. It makes many of these
ideals *easier* to find outside marriage. And even if companionate
bonds would be impaired without some public status, it does
not follow that they would be impaired without *legal* status.
Remarkably, then, one of the most common and powerfully felt
objections to conjugal marriage policy is also one of the easiest
to answer. The law simply has much less to do with this than
people commonly suppose. We can unpack this.

Note first that, however the marriage debate is resolved, two
men or two women will be free to live together, with or without

a sexual relationship or a wedding ceremony. Meanwhile, prison will still await bigamists. The same-sex civil marriage debate is not about anyone's private behavior, but about legal recognition. The decision to honor conjugal marriage *bans nothing*.

But neither does it *discourage* companionship. In fact, it would be a failure of moral and spiritual imagination to suppose that companionate ideals could not be realized even in deep nonmarital bonds (see chapter 4 on nonmarital friendship). Not recognizing certain relationships as civil marriages will not make people lonelier unless we embrace the revisionist idea that emotional intimacy is what sets marriage apart, so that it is socially unacceptable to seek companionship outside it. Here too, then, the answer is to promote, not suppress, the conjugal view; to oppose the revisionist conception of marriage as simply the closest of bonds.* The conjugal view *liberates* us for companionship.

This begins to address the oft-raised question of what unmarried people should *do*, given the special personal value of marriage. Like anyone else, they should have deep and fulfilling relationships. They should have the finest ales and best steaks, if they please. They should pursue art, adventure, service, ministry or music or writing or any of a thousand other ways of adding to the world's sums of beauty and love. They, like anyone else, should live richly and give freely. In no two cases will that mean the same thing; in *none* would conjugal marriage laws ban anyone's options.

Of course, we all need community, and in this respect some people will know more hardship than others. Thus young peo-

---

*Many same-sex-attracted people who do not support legally recognizing same-sex unions have explored the special value for themselves of deep friendships. See, e.g., John Heard, "Dreadtalk: 'Holy Sex and Christian Friendship' John Heard —Life Week 2009 at the University of Sydney—Remarks," *Dreadnoughts*, May 4, 2009, http://johnheard.blogspot.com/2009/02/dreadtalk-holy-sex-christian -friendship.html. See also Eve Tushnet, "Gay and Catholic: What the Church Gets Right and Wrong about Being Gay," http://onfaith.washingtonpost.com/on faith/guestvoices/2010/10/gay_and_catholic_what_the_church_gets_right_and_ wrong_about_being_gay.html, and, generally, http://eve-tushnet.blogspot.com/.

ple experiencing same-sex desire can face isolation as their peers first awaken to the opposite sex; confusion about their own emergent feelings; humiliation by bullies, if they say too much; and the black burden of a secret, if they do not. Parents, teachers, and friends must be sensitive to these struggles.

As relatives, coworkers, and neighbors, we must remember that social hardship isn't limited to youth. *Whatever* keeps some people from legally recognized relationships—under *whatever* marriage policy—we should fight arbitrary or abusive treatment of them with the same force and diligence with which we would oppose unjust distinctions by race or sex. People left dry by isolation of *any* kind we should graft onto other forms of community—as friends, fellow worshippers, neighbors, close partners in common causes, de facto members of our families and big siblings to our children, and natural and regular guests in our homes.

One could do all these things—and indeed, if one chose, promote homosexual unions as a path to personal fulfillment—and still favor recognizing only male-female unions as civil marriages. David Blankenhorn explicitly affirms "the equal dignity of homosexual love" in one of the most prominent books defending traditional marriage laws.*[7] A relationship may be of the greatest worth without calling for state recognition—especially if recognizing it would have harmful side effects, as Blankenhorn thinks that redefined civil marriage would have for children.

As for the concern that traditional marriage law, if it does not ban or discourage companionship, at least impairs certain forms of it by robbing companions of public acknowledgment:

---

*Though Blankenhorn recently wrote that "the time has come for me to accept gay marriage," he reiterated that he retracts nothing from his book, and even reaffirmed—and lamented—that "gay marriage has become a significant contributor to marriage's continuing deinstitutionalization"; David Blankenhorn, "How My View on Gay Marriage Changed," *New York Times*, June 22, 2012, http://www.nytimes.com/2012/06/23/opinion/how-my-view-on-gay-marriage-changed.html?_r=0.

People rightly take delight in the public knowledge of their bonds, and not just the romantic ones. Nicknames and team names, idioms and inside jokes, outings and co-hostings, joint projects and pacts all serve as much to make a friendship public as to build it up. Yet no one proposes to recognize friendships by law. For it is clear that publicity, which may well matter to our bonds, does not require *legal* status; and even among worthy bonds, the state must keep clear distinctions where blurring them would harm the common good.

Finally, you might want the law not just to get out of companionship's way, but to incentivize it. But among all the forms that companionship can take, which should it single out, and why? Legal recognition makes sense only where *regulation* does: these are inseparable. The law, which deals in generalities, can regulate only relationships with a definite structure. Such regulation is justified only where more than private interests are at stake, and where it would not obscure distinctions between bonds that the common good relies on. As we have argued, the only romantic bond that meets these criteria is marriage, *conjugal* marriage.

ᴑ   ᴑ   ᴑ

Perhaps by now our answer to this objection seems to prove too much. If same-sex partners' material needs can be met, if their equal social dignity can be upheld, if various of their bonds can even enjoy publicity, one might ask, what difference could it make whether their relationships are *legally* recognized? What good do conjugal marriage supporters hope to accomplish by withholding just that?

But to ask this is to assume, mistakenly, that the conjugal view is concerned with targeting same-sex relationships. It is the redefinition of marriage, not any particular conferral of benefits, that concerns us. What we wish to avoid is the harm this does to the common good.

This brings us to the point with which we began this book. Our argument here has not been about homosexuality, as important and disputed as that subject is. In the first and last analysis, what we have debated—what we have defended—is marriage.

ℒ 7 ℒ

Conclusion

Would enshrining the conjugal view violate moral or religious neutrality? We consider this objection last for a reason. By now, as promised in the Introduction, we have made a case for upholding or restoring the conjugal view of marriage and have addressed many theoretical and practical objections to it, without any appeal to revelation or religious authority. This reflects a crucial difference between marriage and religious dogma and practice: doctrines of the Trinity or the Incarnation, the enlightenment of the Buddha, baptisms, bar mitzvahs, fasting, and prayer. Unlike these matters, the human good of marriage and its bearing on the common good can be understood, analyzed, and discussed without engaging anyone's theology.

Most religions do have ceremonies for recognizing marriages and teach the conjugal view, or something very much like it. Many people are motivated to support the conjugal view for reasons that include religious ones. But the same goes for the revisionist view. So these facts cannot settle which view should be enshrined in law.

Even so, some would say, to enshrine the conjugal view, as many societies have done for ages, is to privilege what is today a controversial moral belief. Again, this argument would equally exclude the revisionist view. Both views make claims about which relationships to honor and encourage as marriages— and, by implication, which relationships not to recognize in this way. The revisionist view, at least in the version currently most represented in public debates, would honor and privilege both monogamous heterosexual and same-sex unions but not polyamorous ones. And both views are disputed. There is no neutral marriage policy.

But that is true not only of marriage. Settling other policies also requires controversial moral stances on issues where theologies clash: affirmative action, abortion, assisted suicide and euthanasia, poverty relief, capital punishment, torture, nuclear deterrence, and more. That does not mean that the state must keep silent on these matters. It does mean that citizens owe it to each other to explain the reasons for their views with clarity and candor, as we have tried to do here.

ɔ   ɔ   ɔ

A thought experiment will crystallize our central argument.

Almost every culture in every time and place has had some institution that resembles what we know as marriage. But imagine that human beings reproduced asexually and that human offspring were born self-sufficient. In that case, would any culture have developed an institution anything like what we know as marriage? It is clear that the answer is no.

Our view explains why. If human beings reproduced asexually, organic bodily union would be impossible; no kind of union would have any special relationship to bearing and rearing children; and the norms that these two realities require would be at best optional features of any relationship, to be observed or not according to taste. Thus, the essential features of marriage— those of comprehensive union—would be missing; there would be no human need that marriage uniquely filled.

The insight that pair bonds make little sense and *uniquely* answer to no human need apart from mind-body unions inherently ordered to family life merely underscores the conclusions for which we have argued: marriage is a kind of union shaped by its comprehensiveness and thus, among other things, fulfilled by procreation and childrearing. Only this can account for its essential features, which make less sense in other relationships. Because marriage uniquely meets essential needs in such a structured way, it should be regulated for the common good, which can be understood apart from specifically religious arguments. The needs of those who cannot prudently or who do not marry (even owing to naturally occurring factors), and whose relationships are thus justifiably regarded as different in kind, can be met in other ways.

The view laid out in this book is thus not a cynical trade-off between the good of a few adults and everyone else. Nor are there "mere arguments" squaring off against people's "concrete needs." We reject both of these dichotomies. Marriage understood as the conjugal union of husband and wife really serves the good of children, the good of spouses, and the common good of society. When the arguments against this view fail, the arguments for it succeed, and the arguments against its alternative are decisive, we take this as evidence of the truth of the conjugal view. For reason is not just a debater's tool for idly refracting positions into premises, but a lens for bringing into focus the features of human flourishing.

Further Reflections on Bodily Union

Much of our argument turns on what we call organic bodily union, so it is important to address objections to it.[1] Here we consider questions about the coherence and relevance of this concept.

We apply the concept of organic bodily union in the following passage from chapter 2:

> In coitus, and there alone, a man and a woman's bodies participate by virtue of their sexual complementarity in a coordination that has the biological purpose of reproduction—a function that neither can perform alone. Their coordinated action is, biologically, the first step (the behavioral part) of the reproductive process. By engaging in it, they are united, and do not merely touch, much as one's heart, lungs, and other organs are united: by coordinating toward a biological good of the whole that they form together. Here the whole is the couple; the single biological good, their reproduction.

In short, our argument is that marriage comprehensively unites persons: this means, among other things, that it unites them in all their basic dimensions. But persons are embodied, so marriage includes bodily union. Two organs unite by coordinating for a biological end (survival) of the whole they compose together (an organism); likewise, two people unite bodily by coordinating toward a biological end (reproduction) of the whole they compose as a couple. Only in the generative act do two people thus become "one flesh" to seal a marriage. More precisely, only in coitus do two people realize part of an inherently coordinated bodily process—or thus unite bodily and maritally.

Some have objected quite generally that the concept of bodily union is gerrymandered. It either includes too much (e.g., solitary sexual acts) or excludes too much (e.g., coitus involving a partner who is missing gonads). But an individual's climax alone is too thin an event to count as *coordination* of *two people*. Male-female coitus, by contrast, inherently involves two. And it *remains* a stage of the coordinated process of reproduction when conditions accidental or external to the act (such as the absence of an internal organ) keep the process from reaching completion. But non-coital sex acts (between two men, two women, or a man and a woman) form *no* stage of the process of bodily coordination toward reproduction, or anything else; they are not bodily unions; thus they are not marital acts.

Barry Deutsch has attempted to develop this criticism on the *FamilyScholars* blog. He writes:

> 1) Individual adults are naturally incomplete with respect to sexual reproduction.
> 2) Reproduction can only be begun via coitus between a man and a woman.
> 3) Thus, during coitus, a woman and a man's bodies are biologically united and become one flesh.
> How does #3 follow from #1 and #2? Answer: It doesn't.[2]

Deutsch claims that our argument is a *non sequitur* because there is "no *non*-metaphorical sense in which the spouses become 'one flesh'" in light of the fact that "the man and the woman . . . remain two separate entities," as can be confirmed by a "DNA sampling."

It is Deutsch's claim against us that is a *non sequitur*. Deutsch seems to assume that a man and a woman's common biological action cannot make them biologically united at all (united in any respect), unless it makes them completely so (united in every respect). This is clearly false. Organic unity can be genuine without being all-encompassing: two organisms can be organically united for some purposes while remaining separate and self-sufficient in other respects. Whether we are talking about humans or zebras, individual members of a mammalian species are separate and self-sufficient with respect to locomotion, digestion, respiration, and most other functions. With respect to reproduction, however, individual members are not self-sufficient. A male or female is half of a potential mated pair whose biological (and, as such, organic) common action—or unity—in coitus characteristically produces offspring.

Deutsch's appeal to "DNA sampling" as evidence that there is "no *non*-metaphorical sense" in which males and females organically unite in mating is unsound. Genetic identity is not what constitutes biological unity (consider identical twins)— nor is it, as we will show, even necessary for biological unity of every meaningful sort. Elsewhere Deutsch suggests that biological unity requires being "physically joined." But physical joining just in itself can scarcely be considered a meaningful kind of bodily unity, since it may well include the "unions" of animals that are tied to each other by the tails, or whose hides have been surgically attached at a point. There would be nothing morally significant about these instances of "physical joining."

The rest of Deutsch's posting is ostensibly an effort to find such a sense in which coitus is a real bodily union. But he need not have looked very far. Our answer was in the very passage that he first quotes: "they are biologically united . . . *similarly to the way in which one's heart, lungs, and other organs form a unity: by coordinating for the biological good of the whole.*"[3]

Thus, following Aristotle, we argue that *coordination toward a common biological end* unites two people bodily. This conception clearly allows for *partial* biological unity, in respect of coordination toward *some* but not *other* biological ends.

Think of a biological function in humans. Now think of the parts that naturally play a role in serving that function and can thus be said to be coordinated together toward its fulfillment. Our claim is that there is one meaningful sense in which the parts just mentioned enjoy a biological unity, precisely *by virtue* of that coordination toward a common biological function.

If the function that you thought of was locomotion, metabolism, respiration, or one of many others, then the parts that you thought of were organs within a single individual; and the function itself played some role in serving that individual's biological life. But if reproduction was the function you picked, then the parts that you thought of were not organs in a single individual; and the function in question was one that served the biological good of a male-female pair as a whole: their reproduction. Coitus is the process by which such coordination toward a common biological function—such real, if limited, biological unity—is achieved.*

---

*What about artificial reproduction? Recall that we base our general formulation of bodily union ("mutual coordination of the parts toward a biological good of the whole") on an analogy to the union of organs in an individual organism. But the same analogy allows us to make this formulation more precise. After all, the heart and lungs form one body not just by coordinating toward the biological good of a single organism's life, but by doing so *in the way that they are biologically ordered to doing so* (as captured by the familiar medical-scientific idea of a biological system "functioning properly"). Thus, if an organ plays its characteristic *role* but not in its characteristic *way* (say, a heart-like object causes circulation, but only by making sounds that trigger a machine to pump blood), it is not as truly united with the other organs to form a single whole. Likewise, two people (and it is usually more) are not really united bodily if they cooperate to produce a human being by artificial reproduction—not because there is something wrong with medical technology, but because there is something distinctive about bodily union, and natural joint action is integral to *that*. Moreover, gametes that have been extracted and manipulated for laboratory use are hardly parts of the parents' persons, so combining them could not possibly make for a bodily (hence personal) union of the parents, as their bodily coordination in coitus does.

Deutsch objects that "it's not true that every part of our body is 'coordinated' . . . for a common biological purpose . . . [namely] biological life," and cites hair, skin tags, and benign tumors. But these examples support our point. Hair, skin tags, and benign tumors—though contiguous with our bodies—are not biologically united with them in just the way that, say, a heart and lungs are. To remove tumors or skin tags (or any given hair) has no effect on our organic functioning; that is precisely why doing so is not *mutilation*. (In Deutsch's own words, "they could all be removed at no biological cost.") If there is still a sense in which they are parts of one's body—because of their contiguity with it—that just shows that there are different (more and less important) senses in which two things can be united. But that is no strike against our argument, since we articulated precisely which sense we meant.

Deutsch continues:

> I largely agree with George that a marriage, in nearly all cases, requires a physical, sexual union to become complete. (There may be individual couples who are exceptions, but for the overwhelming majority of couples, it will not feel like a true marriage without a sexual union.)

It is not clear what Deutsch means here. If marriage is a human good with some essential features that hold regardless of the participants, then either consummation is one such essential, or it is not. If it is, then Deutsch's second sentence is false; if it is not, then his first sentence is puzzling. If, on the other hand, Deutsch thinks that there are no essential features of marriage that hold constant across would-be spouses, then we wonder why he thinks that marriage would require even mutual commitment (much less monogamous or exclusive commitment). Why, too, would he not think that such a malleable good would be hindered by legal recognition, which imposes uniform constraints on every recognized marriage?

Perhaps, then, Deutsch means that a certain sort of mutual pleasuring is essential to marital unity, and that this is what most (but not all) couples achieve through sex. But here again, we have argued that pleasure cannot be another biological good in respect of which two individuals are biologically united by sexual activities other than coitus:

> Pleasure cannot play this role for several reasons. The good must be truly common and for the couple as a whole, but pleasures (and, indeed, any psychological good) are private and benefit partners, if at all, only individually. The good must be bodily, but pleasures are aspects of experience. The good must be inherently valuable, but pleasures are not as such good in themselves—witness, for example, sadistic pleasures.[4]

Ignoring our first two points, Deutsch says of the last sentence:

> [That] is a little like saying "childbirth is not as such a good in itself—witness, for example, the birth of Hitler." For any good, one could imagine an instance of the good being used for negative purposes; yet if "can never be used for negative purposes" is the definition of good, then absolutely nothing on this mortal Earth is or ever can be good. That's silly. In the right context (i.e., not Hitler), childbirth is a good; and in the right context, sexual pleasure is also a good.

Our point is not that sadistic pleasures are inherently good things that just happen to be used for bad purposes. First, it is a confusion to speak of sadistic pleasures being *used for* bad purposes. It is the other way around: sadists seek what is bad or evil for the sake of pleasure, which they seek, presumably, for its own sake. Second, we agree that good things can be twisted.

Our point was that in sadistic pleasures, it is not as if the pleasure itself is good, only sought by illicit means. Pleasure taken in bad things is *bad*. And we doubt that Deutsch would disagree. If a man took pleasure in strolling the halls of a pediatric oncology ward to watch children die of cancer, no one would say, "Well, it's too bad that's what suits his fancy—but at least he got pleasure out of it." Pleasure, considered as a state of mind, independently of its object, does not have its own value; it shares in the moral quality of that object. Now communities—like friendship or marriage—are built up by the pursuit of what is inherently valuable. So marriage cannot be built up by the common pursuit of pleasure just as such. Spouses must achieve some good (organic union as an embodiment of their commitment), in which the pleasure they take is then an additional perfection. That was our point.

From these misunderstandings, Deutsch rushes to his conclusion:

> But at heart, "What Is Marriage" is a faith-based argument. George believes, as a matter of faith (all he has, since he lacks evidence), that there's something called "bodily union," a biological merger of male and female bodies, that occurs only in coitus. . . .
>
> But basing laws on Robert George's faith in a mythical "bodily union" is no better than basing laws on my faith in Mork from Ork. Robert George and his fellow-travelers may have faith in magical bodily unions, but they would be morally wrong to force that faith on us through the legal system. . . .
>
> But now we're treading on even more bewildering territory. Do we want a society in which people's civil rights are decided, not by what is just, not by what is pragmatic, not by what is fair, but by a metaphor? Metaphors, unlike facts, can change arbitrarily. Suppose that George chooses to believe in a different metaphor next year—a

metaphor saying that comprehensive unity can only be achieved by dog owners, for instance. Would we then be obliged to change marriage laws to exclude cat owners?

Ridicule is the last resort of desperate arguments. If Deutsch had really grasped our view and produced a valid argument against it, he would have had no need of putting words into our mouths ("biological merger") or festooning his critique with dismissive terms ("mythical," "magical"). A good objection would have sufficed. But a dozen sneers do not make an objection.

What Deutsch calls the protean "myth" at the heart of marriage law has been its cornerstone for centuries. Our legal tradition understood coitus and coitus alone as consummating (and thus completing) a marriage, but never accepted infertility as a ground for annulment or dissolution. Our argument can make ample sense of that tradition in a way that also accounts for other marital norms (such as permanence and exclusivity). Can Deutsch? What is the nonarbitrary basis on which he would ground *these* norms (assuming he accepts them), while rejecting sexual complementarity as integral to marriage?

The common biological action of mating is no myth; it is a fact. Ask any zoologist or farmer. The real question is whether human mating, precisely by virtue of the unity it achieves, is capable of having moral significance of a certain sort. Can it embody and complete an inherently valuable, comprehensive form of relationship—historically known as marriage—that is, like mating itself, ordered to procreation? We have argued as much. If we are correct, then not only sexual complementarity, but the other structuring marital principles that are recognized by our legal tradition—such as sexual exclusivity and the pledge of fidelity "till death do us part" (rather than, say, "for as long as love lasts")—are intelligible and sound.

It is true that if marriage requires bodily union, then certain (sets of) people who want to form a marriage (together) cannot.[5] But that is true *of every view of marriage.* Every plausible view will also allow that they can, given sufficient maturity, form (with each other) loving and sustaining relationships of other types, and should.

Of course, if marriage is a good, then in a sense it is bad if one's view implies impediments to it. But it is important to remember that the badness would be in the *impediments*, not the view itself—assuming the latter remained defensible given all the evidence. Similarly, it is no strike against the revisionist view that it "excludes" from marriage people lacking, say, the psychological ability, or freedom from responsibilities, to make new long-term commitments.

Moreover, that badness is not as great as the revisionist thinks. For revisionists, marriage differs from other bonds by degree—as the most valuable or deepest kind of communion—so those who do not marry just settle for *less*. On the conjugal view, for which marriage is the paradigm of fulfillment of one *type* of intimacy among others, there are several basic types of love, each with its own characteristic scale and forms of depth and mutual presence and care. So the unmarried are not denied the pinnacle of social fulfillment.

Furthermore, this badness—seen in its true proportions, traced to its true causes—does not point up a new *kind* of difficulty for the conjugal (or any other) view. If a person's psychology makes marriage imprudent or unworkable, it is not any less bad that another person who cannot find a mate cannot marry, or that an only child tied up caring for her ailing mother cannot marry. These are all people of equal dignity for whom marriage would be a real fulfillment but is practically impossible through no fault of their own.

They may yet *want* something else that involves romantic feeling and domestic life. And one can have a kind of sweeping friendship that involves those elements. What we argue is that comprehensive union is crucial to making sense of the desirability and fittingness of the *combination* of these and other characteristic features of marriage, and thus of the distinctive value of whatever basic good (besides friendship) is on offer in their vicinity. And that treating fragments of this good as if they were the whole will make it harder for us to see (and live out) their unity. On this, as we have seen, candid revisionists increasingly agree: if sexual complementarity is optional, so are just about all the other distinctively marital norms.

o   o   o

Analyzing bodily union in such detail might well leave you a bit cold, and wondering what the moral significance of such fine distinctions could be. This might suggest that you reject, not this particular standard of bodily union, but the idea that bodily union *however understood* could matter in itself and not just for its emotional effects. Against this, we have argued that the body is a real part of the person, so that extending two people's unity along their bodily dimension could *itself* have personal and moral significance; and that no other view can explain why only sex can consummate a marriage.

But the very same reaction could have a different cause entirely—a natural fatigue that, being common after any close analysis, would not reflect on the merits of *this* one. Everyone knows, for example, that consent is critical to the morality of sexual interactions. But if we spent thousands of words splicing the fine distinctions between what does and does not count as consent (and there are some very hard cases), we might similarly be left cold, and in need of reminding ourselves—by zooming back out, so to speak—just why consent mattered in the first place.

We might also be tempted to think that anyone who conducted such a careful investigation of consent thought that it was *all* that mattered, but this, too, would be a mistake. Likewise, it would be a mistake to infer, from these fine distinctions about what counts as real bodily union, any abandonment (in principle *or* practice) of the integrated view of human beings as body-mind wholes.[6] In fact, it is just the opposite: we have paid the concept of bodily union more attention precisely because we think that both mental-spiritual and bodily unity are critical to marriage, and that people have recently relaxed attention to the latter.

Keeping all this in mind, one can indeed—as for centuries, people did—see something morally distinctive, even awe-inspiring, and crucial for marriage, in the sort of human act that unites generation to generation as one blood, and man to woman as one flesh.

Afterword

Ryan T. Anderson and Robert P. George

A decade ago, when we began work on *What Is Marriage?*, President Obama affirmed that marriage unites a man and a woman. So did forty-five states and the federal government. The only states to redefine marriage had done so through activist court rulings or, in 2009, legislative action. At the ballot box, citizens had uniformly voted against redefinition. Most agreed with Obama.

Then, in 2012, Obama "evolved," and the Supreme Court took cases involving marriage law. Nothing in the Constitution answered the actual question at hand—what is marriage?—so the Court should have left the issue to the people. But in 2013, it struck down the federal definition of marriage as a male-female union in a 5–4 ruling. And it punted on a challenge to a *state* definition of marriage adopted in a 2008 constitutional referendum by which a majority of Californians—yes, Californians—overturned an activist court. Only in 2015 did the Supreme Court, breaking 5–4 again, redefine marriage for the nation, provoking four irrefutable dissents.

"Same-sex marriage" advocates told the public that they sought only the "freedom to marry." Never mind that in all

---

This essay originally appeared in *USA Today* on January 1, 2020.

fifty states, same-sex couples were already free to live as they chose. Legal recognition was about the definition of marriage for all of society. It was about affirmation—by the government and everyone else. It is unsurprising, then, that a campaign crying "live and let live," once it prevailed, quickly began shutting down Catholic adoption agencies and harassing evangelical bakers and florists. What this shows is that it was never about "live and let live"; it was a merely a tactical stance.

While these were the early effects of redefinition, the more profound consequences will be to marriage itself. Law shapes culture; culture shapes beliefs; beliefs shape action. The law now teaches that mothers and fathers are replaceable; that marriage is simply about consenting adult relationships, of whatever size or shape the parties happen to prefer. This undermines the truth that every child deserves a mother and a father—one of each. It also undercuts any reasonable justification for marital norms. After all, if marriage is about romantic connection, period, why require monogamy? There's nothing magical about the number two, as defenders of "polyamory" point out. If marriage isn't a conjugal union uniting a man and a woman as one flesh, why should it involve sexual exclusivity? If it isn't a comprehensive union inherently ordered to childbearing and -rearing, why should it be permanent or pledged to permanence? The marriage redefiners could not answer these questions when challenged to show that the elimination of sexual complementarity did not undermine other marital norms. Today they increasingly admit that they have no stake in upholding norms of monogamy, exclusivity, and permanence.

Same-sex marriage didn't create these problems. Large segments of society had unwisely already gone along with the erosion of marital norms in the wake of the Sexual Revolution—with the rise of the hook-up culture, cohabitation, nonmarital childbearing, and no-fault divorce. It was no surprise that many would then question the relevance of the male–female norm. Legal redefinition is a consequence of the cultural breakdown of marriage.

But it will now be a catalyst for further erosion. Already we see respectable opinion makers mainstreaming "throuples," "ethical nonmonogamy," and "open relationships." This was predictable; we and others predicted it.

What we didn't predict were the headlines about transgender and nonbinary "identities." A decade ago, few Americans had given much thought to the "T" in "LGBT." Today, transgender identity dominates the discussion of sexuality and sexual morality. There's a logic here. If we can't see the point of our sexual embodiment where it matters most—in marriage—we'll question if it matters at all, hence the push to see gender as "fluid" and as "existing along a spectrum" of nonbinary options.

There's a deeper logic, too. Implicit in the push for same-sex marriage was body–self dualism: the idea that we're actually nonphysical entities inhabiting physical bodies—"ghosts in machines." That's why "the arrangement of the plumbing" in sexual acts seemed not to matter. True one-flesh union, the foundation and matrix of conjugal marriage, was thought illusory. What mattered was emotional union and partners' use of their bodies to induce desirable sensations and feelings. Of course, two men or two women (or throuples, or even larger sexual ensembles) could do that. But the logic didn't stay with marriage. If the body is mere "plumbing," then sex matters less than "gender identity."

This has had tragic consequences, especially for children. Nearly unthinkable a decade ago, it's now common practice among certain medical professionals to tell children experiencing gender dysphoria that they are "trapped in the wrong body," even that their bodies are merely "Pop-Tart foil packets," to quote one expert. Doctors now prescribe puberty-blocking drugs to otherwise healthy children struggling to accept their bodies. They prescribe cross-sex hormones for young teens to transform their bodies to "align with" their "gender identities." They perform double mastectomies on adolescent girls—with two such operations being performed on thirteen-year-olds as part of a taxpayer-funded National Institutes of Health study.

These changes weren't grassroots movements. They've come from people wielding political, economic, and cultural power to advance sexual-liberationist ideology. It's been top-down change—from Hollywood's portrayal of LGBT characters to business executives boycotting states over religious-freedom laws. Having lost at the ballot box over and over—even in California— activists found new avenues: ideologically friendly courts, federal agencies, big corporations. Having secured a judicial redefinition of marriage, they pivoted to the "T," with the Obama administration redefining "sex" to mean "gender identity" and imposing new policy on all schools. And having won government support, activists turned to eliminating private dissent. Beto O'Rourke wants to yank the tax exemption of noncompliant churches. Tim Gill vows to spend his fortune to "punish the wicked." Who are "the wicked"? They are those who refuse to accept the new sexual orthodoxy.

All of us, including those identifying as LGBT, are made in God's image, are endowed with profound dignity, and thus deserve respect. It's because of this dignity and out of such respect that the institutions serving the human good—like the marriage-based family—should be supported, not undermined or redefined; that basic rights like religious freedom ought to be upheld, not infringed; that a healthy moral and physical ecology —especially for children—must be preserved. The "progress" of the past decade has exacted steep costs.

Notes

INTRODUCTION

1. For ease of reading, we have transposed quotations from the poem into modern English.

2. See John M. Finnis, "Law, Morality, and 'Sexual Orientation,'" *Notre Dame Law Review* 69 (1994): 1049, 1066; John Finnis, "Marriage: A Basic and Exigent Good," *The Monist* 91 (July/October 2008): 388–406. See also Patrick Lee and Robert P. George, *Body-Self Dualism in Contemporary Ethics and Politics* (Cambridge and New York: Cambridge University Press, 2008), 176–97.

3. See Stephen Macedo, "Homosexuality and the Conservative Mind," *Georgetown Law Journal* 84 (1995): 261, 279.

4. See Mark Oppenheimer, "A Gay Catholic Voice against Same-Sex Marriage," *New York Times,* June 4, 2010, http://www.nytimes .com/2010/06/05/us/05beliefs.html. For the provocative and beautiful reflections of the woman about whom that article was written, see Eve Tushnet's blog at http://eve-tushnet.blogspot.com/. See also http://www.washingtonpost.com/opinions/why-i-oppose-gay -marriage/2012/09/21/1cd0056c-02a2-11e2-91e7-2962c74e7738_ story.html?socialreader_check=0&denied=1. And see John Heard's fresh and moving account of his evolution toward the conjugal view at his blog, *Dreadnought: Out of Shadows into Truth*, archived at http://johnheard.blogspot.com/.

CHAPTER 1: CHALLENGES TO REVISIONISTS

1. John Corvino and Maggie Gallagher, *Debating Same-Sex Marriage* (New York: Oxford Paperbacks), 15.

2. It is not merely that we and revisionists are talking about different relationships by the same name. For we can describe the dispute without using the word "marriage": Most agree that there is a certain kind of relationship that is inherently sexual, and uniquely enriched by family life; and that it uniquely requires permanent and exclusive commitment to begin at all. Our thesis is that the basic human good that answers to these descriptions is one that only a man and a woman can form together.

3. See Maggie Gallagher, "(How) Will Gay Marriage Weaken Marriage as a Social Institution: A Reply to Andrew Koppelman," *University of St. Thomas Law Journal* 2 (2004): 33, 51–52.

4. Kevin Noble Maillard, "Beyond Marriage, Blood, or Adoption," *New York Times*, February 15, 2012, http://www.nytimes.com/roomfordebate/2012/02/13/family-ties-without-tying-the-knot/beyond-marriage-blood-or-adoption.

5. Molly Young, "He and He and He," *New York Magazine*, July 29, 2012, http://nymag.com/news/features/sex/2012/benny-morecock-throuple/.

6. Susan Donaldson James, "Polyamory on the Rise among Divorce-Disgusted Americans," *ABC News*, December 8, 2011, http://abcnews.go.com/Health/polyamory-rise-divorce-wary-young-americans/story?id=15107435#.T2ahSRE2-uK.

7. See "Beyond Same-Sex Marriage: A New Strategic Vision For All Our Families and Relationships," BeyondMarriage.org, July 26, 2006, http://beyondmarriage.org/full_statement.html.

8. Jessica Bennett, "Only You. And You. And You: Polyamory—Relationships with Multiple, Mutually Consenting Partners—Has a Coming-Out Party," *Newsweek*, July 29, 2009, http://www.newsweek.com/2009/07/28/only-you-and-you-and-you.html.

9. "Three-Person Civil Union Sparks Controversy in Brazil," *BBC News*, August 28, 2012, http://www.bbc.co.uk/news/world-latin-america-19402508.

10. "Mexico City Proposes Temporary Marriage Licenses," *The Telegraph*, September 30, 2011, http://www.telegraph.co.uk/news/worldnews/centralamericaandthecaribbean/mexico/8798982/Mexico-City-proposes-temporary-marriage-licences.html.

11. "Toronto School District Board Promotes Polygamy, Group Sex to Children," http://blazingcatfur.blogspot.com/2012/09/tdsb-promotes-polygamy-group-sex-to-children.html.

12. Elizabeth Brake, "Minimal Marriage: What Political Liberalism Implies for Marriage Law," *Ethics* 120 (2010): 303.

13. See, for example, Robert P. George, "Same-Sex Marriage and John Rauch," *First Things*, August 10, 2006, http://www.firstthings .com/onthesquare/2006/08/same-sex-marriage-and-jon-rauc, which is a reply to Jonathan Rauch, "Not So Fast, Mr. George," *Independent Gay Forum*, August 2, 2006, http://igfculturewatch .com/2006/08/02/not-so-fast-mr-george/.

CHAPTER 2: COMPREHENSIVE UNION

1. See, for example, David Braine, *The Human Person: Animal and Spirit* (Notre Dame, Ind.: University of Notre Dame Press, 1994).

2. Though we are essentially body-mind composites, all our unions do not extend equally on both planes. Silently consenting to an agreement unites people; a marital act unites people. And plainly, the latter involves bodily union as the former does not, even though neither unites *mere* minds or *mere* bodies.

3. The following discussion owes much to the work of Germain Grisez and Alexander Pruss.

4. See, e.g., Thomas Laqueur, *Making Sex: Body and Gender from the Greeks to Freud* (Cambridge, Mass.: Harvard University Press, 1990), 48.

5. For more on this philosophical point, see Lee and George, *Body-Self Dualism* (cited in Introduction, n. 2), 95–115, 176–97.

6. One of the definitions in the *Oxford English Dictionary* for "consummation" is "[t]he completion of marriage by sexual intercourse"; *Oxford English Dictionary*, 2nd ed. (Oxford: Clarendon Press of Oxford University Press, 1989), 3:803. The earliest such usage recorded in English law was the 1548 Act 2–3 Edw. VI, c. 23 § 2: "Sentence for Matrimony, commanding Solemnization, Cohabitation, Consummation and Tractation as becometh Man and Wife to have"; ibid. The Act was carrying forward into English a set of legal principles in force for many centuries in England, though largely in Latin legal language. In more modern usage, "consummation of marriage" is still regarded in family law as "[t]he first post-marital act of sexual intercourse between a husband and wife." *Black's Law Dictionary*, 9th ed. (St. Paul, Minn.: West, 2009), 359.

7. See Kenji Yoshino, "The Best Argument against Gay Marriage: And Why It Fails," *Slate*, December 13, 2010, http://www.slate .com/articles/news_and_politics/jurisprudence/2010/12/the_best_ argument_against_gay_marriage.html.

8. Of course, our scoring conventions are what make hitting the ball ordered to winning games, whereas coitus is ordered to reproduction by nature, by the biological facts. So coitus remains coordination toward reproduction, *whatever* the spouses' beliefs about conception, even if (say) a team no longer counts as playing baseball if new scoring rules make winning impossible. Recall, too, that mating (*behavior*) is necessary, not sufficient, for a marital *act*. For that, spouses must be choosing this behavior to embody their comprehensive union—and thus, for example, unwilling to seek it with others.

9. This does not mean that marriage is, or should be—or even can be—the most intensive or extensive sort of union in every respect; we distinguish that view, and argue against it, to some extent later in this chapter, and in greater detail in Sherif Girgis, "Real Marriage," *National Review*, March 21, 2011, http://www.national review.com/articles/263679/real-marriage-sherif-girgis. Moreover, it is true that any two people, not just a man and a woman—indeed, not just two men in love, but two brothers, a father and son, and so on—*can* coordinate all activities and share a home. But because their union cannot be sealed by the conjugal act, and is not inherently ordered to family life, it does not objectively *call for* such broad domestic sharing. People in other bonds may opt for the same, but it is not normative for them.

10. *The Book of Common Prayer* (1662), The Form of Solemnization of Matrimony; the phrase quoted is from the pledging of troth (vow) by the man to the woman and the woman to the man.

11. We are not inferring that *x* is a property of marriage, from the fact that something like *x* is a property of bodily union. We are pointing to parallels and harmonies among the three ways in which marriage is comprehensive (in its distinctive acts, goods, and commitment), to highlight the unity of the conjugal view, thus bolstering it. Why comprehensive in *these* three respects? Because if bonds fundamentally *are* commitments to pursue certain goods following certain norms, then these features are what give different *types* of bonds their distinctive character and value. Thus, again, marriage is comprehensive in some basic ways, not in every sense. But the same holds of most revisionists' master principle: a spouse cannot be your "number one partner" in *every* activity, or your "soul-mate" in *every* domain.

12. On the importance of stability in children's lives, see, for instance, Shannon E. Cavanagh, "Family Structure History and Adolescent Adjustment," *Journal of Family Issues* 30 (September 1, 2009):

1265, http://jfi.sagepub.com/content/29/7/944.short. For a study showing the importance of fidelity for marital stability, see Paul R. Amato and Stacy J. Rogers, "A Longitudinal Study of Marital Problems and Subsequent Divorce," *Journal of Marriage and the Family* 59 (August 1997): 612–24, http://www.jstor.org/stable/353949.

CHAPTER 3: THE STATE AND MARRIAGE

1. Corvino and Gallagher, *Debating Same-Sex Marriage* (cited in chap. 1, n. 1), 96.

2. David Blankenhorn, *The Future of Marriage* (2007; New York: Encounter Books, 2009), 5. Blankenhorn recently announced that "the time has come for me to accept gay marriage." In his announcement, however, he also stated that he stands by all the claims and arguments made in his book—retracting nothing, including the point here quoted.

3. Amy L. Wax, "Diverging Family Structure and 'Rational' Behavior: The Decline in Marriage as a Disorder of Choice," in *Research Handbook on the Economics of Family Law*, edited by Lloyd R. Cohen and Joshua D. Wright, 15–71 (Cheltenham, U.K., and Northampton, Mass.: Elgar, 2011), 59, 61.

4. James Q. Wilson, *The Marriage Problem: How Our Culture Has Weakened Families* (New York: HarperCollins, 2002), 41.

5. Douglas W. Allen and Maggie Gallagher, "Does Divorce Law Affect the Divorce Rate? A Review of Empirical Research, 1995–2006," *IMAPP Research Brief* 1, no. 1 (July 2007), http://www.marriagedebate.com/pdf/imapp.nofault.divrate.pdf.

6. See Jennifer Roback Morse, "Privatizing Marriage Is Impossible," *Public Discourse*, April 2, 2012, http://www.thepublicdiscourse.com/2012/04/5069.

7. United Nations Convention on the Rights of the Child, http://www.unicef.org/crc/.

8. For the relevant studies, see *Marriage and the Public Good: Ten Principles* (Princeton, N.J.: The Witherspoon Institute, 2008), 9–19, http://www.winst.org/family_marriage_and_democracy/WI_Marriage.pdf. This report, signed by some seventy scholars, corroborates the philosophical case for marriage with extensive evidence from the social sciences about the welfare of children and adults.

9. Kristin Anderson Moore, Susan M. Jekielek, and Carol Emig, "Marriage from a Child's Perspective: How Does Family Structure Affect Children, and What Can We Do about It?" *Child Trends Re-*

search Brief (June 2002): 1–2, 6, http://www.childtrends.org/files/MarriageRB602.pdf.

10. Wendy D. Manning and Kathleen A. Lamb, "Adolescent Well-Being in Cohabiting, Married, and Single-Parent Families," *Journal of Marriage and Family* 65, no. 4 (November 2003): 876, 890.

11. See Sara McLanahan, Elisabeth Donahue, and Ron Haskins, "Introducing the Issue," *The Future of Children* 15 (2005): 3; Mary Parke, "Are Married Parents Really Better for Children?: What Research Says about the Effects of Family Structure on Child Well-Being," *CLASP Policy Brief* no. 3 (May 2003); W. Bradford Wilcox, William J. Doherty, Helen Fisher, et al., *Why Marriage Matters: Twenty-Six Conclusions from the Social Sciences*, 2nd ed. (New York: Institute for American Values, 2005), 6.

12. For a discussion of the social science on same-sex parenting, and for studies on the alternative arrangements mentioned here, see chapter 4.

13. *Maynard v. Hill*, 125 U.S. 190, 211 (1888).

14. *Conaway v. Deane*, 903 A.2d 416, 620 (Md. 2007).

15. *Baker v. Baker*, 13 Cal. 87, 103 (1859).

16. *Sharon v. Sharon*, 75 Cal. 1, 33 (1888) (quoting Stewart on *Marriage and Divorce*, sec. 103).

17. *Singer v. Hara*, 522 P.2d 1187, 1195 (Wash. App. 1974).

18. "Nearly all United States Supreme Court decisions declaring marriage to be a fundamental right expressly link marriage to fundamental rights of procreation, childbirth, abortion, and child-rearing." *Andersen v. King County*, 138 P.3d 963, 978 (Wash. 2006). "The family is the basic unit of our society, the center of the personal affections that ennoble and enrich human life. It channels biological drives that might otherwise become socially destructive; it ensures the care and education of children in a stable environment; it establishes continuity from one generation to another; it nurtures and develops the individual initiative that distinguishes a free people. Since the family is the core of our society, the law seeks to foster and preserve marriage." *De Burgh v. De Burgh*, 39 Cal.2d 858, 863–64 (1952). Procreation is "[o]ne of the prime purposes of matrimony." *Maslow v. Maslow*, 117 Cal.App.2d 237, 241 (1953). "Procreation of offspring could be considered one of the major purposes of marriage." *Poe v. Gerstein*, 517 F.2d 787, 796 (5th Cir. 1975).

19. Steven Nock, *Marriage in Men's Lives* (New York: Oxford University Press, 1998).

20. Obviously, none of this is to suggest that any marriage is perfect or that spouses never fail to live up to their vows. We are speaking here in generalities, in light of the accumulated social-scientific evidence.

21. W. Bradford Wilcox and Carlos Cavallé, *The Sustainable Demographic Dividend: What Do Marriage and Fertility Have to Do with the Economy?* (Charlottesville, Va.: The National Marriage Project), http://sustaindemographicdividend.org/articles/the -sustainable-demographic.

22. W. Bradford Wilcox, quoted in H. Brevy Cannon, "New Report: Falling Birth, Marriage Rates Linked to Global Economic Slowdown," October 3, 2011, http://www.virginia.edu/uvatoday/news Release.php?id=16244.

23. Kay S. Hymowitz, *Marriage and Caste in America: Separate and Unequal Families in a Post-Marital Age* (Chicago: Ivan R. Dee, 2006). See also W. Bradford Wilcox, "The Evolution of Divorce," *National Affairs* 1 (2009): 81, 88–93.

24. David Popenoe, *Disturbing the Nest: Family Change and Decline in Modern Societies* (New York: A. de Gruyter, 1988), xiv–xv; Alan Wolfe, *Whose Keeper? Social Science and Moral Obligation* (Berkeley: University of California Press, 1989), 132–42.

25. Isabel V. Sawhill, "Families at Risk," in *Setting National Priorities: The 2000 Election and Beyond*, edited by Henry J. Aaron and Robert D. Reischauer (Washington, D.C.: Brookings Institution Press, 1999), 97, 108; see also *Marriage and the Public Good* (cited above, n. 8), 15.

26. Benjamin Scafidi, *The Taxpayer Costs of Divorce and Unwed Childbearing: First-Ever Estimates for the Nation and for All Fifty States* (New York: Institute for American Values, 2008), http:// www.americanvalues.org/pdfs/COFF.pdf.

27. David Schramm, *Preliminary Estimates of the Economic Consequences of Divorce* (Utah State University, 2003).

28. See, e.g., David Boaz, "Privatize Marriage: A Simple Solution to the Gay-Marriage Debate," *Slate*, April 25, 1997, http://www.slate .com/articles/briefing/articles/1997/04/privatize_marriage.html.

29. See, e.g., William N. Eskridge, Jr., "A History of Same-Sex Marriage," *Virginia Law Review* 79 (1993): 1421–22: "A social constructivist history emphasizes the ways in which marriage is 'constructed' over time, the institution being viewed as reflecting larger social power relations."

30. See ibid., 1434: "[M]arriage is not a naturally generated institution with certain essential elements. Instead it is a construction

that is linked with other cultural and social institutions, so that the old-fashioned boundaries between the public and private life melt away."

31. See *Hernandez v. Robles*, 805 N.Y.S.2d 354, 377 (N.Y. App. Div. 2005) (Saxe, J., dissenting) ("Civil marriage is an institution created by the state. . . ."); and *Andersen v. King County*, 138 P.3d 963, 1018 (Wash. 2006) (Fairhurst, J., dissenting) ("[M]arriage draws its strength from the nature of the civil marriage contract itself and the recognition of that contract by the State.").

32. Andrew Koppelman, "What Marriage Isn't," *Balkinization*, December 18, 2010, http://balkin.blogspot.com/2010/12/what -marriage-isnt.html.

33. Other examples of such basic goods include critical aesthetic appreciation, knowledge, and—to cite another social practice— friendship. See our discussion of basic goods in chapter 2.

34. See John Finnis, "Law, Morality, and 'Sexual Orientation,'" in *Same Sex: Debating the Ethics, Science, and Culture of Homosexuality*, edited by John Corvino, 31–43 (Lanham, Md.: Rowman and Littlefield, 1997). John Finnis, "The Good of Marriage and the Morality of Sexual Relations: Some Philosophical and Historical Observations," *American Journal of Jurisprudence* 42 (1998): 97–134. Both essays are reprinted in *Collected Essays of John Finnis*, vol. 3 (Oxford and New York: Oxford University Press, 2011).

35. Andrew Koppelman, "That Elusive Timeless Essence of Marriage," *Balkinization*, December 31, 2010, http://balkin.blogspot .com/2010/12/that-elusive-timeless-essence-of.html.

36. Bennett, "Only You. And You. And You" (cited in chap. 1, n. 8).

37. Mark Oppenheimer, "Married, with Infidelities," *New York Times*, June 30, 2011, http://www. nytimes.com/2011/07/03/magazine/ infidelity-will-keep-us-together.html?pagewanted=all.

CHAPTER 4: WHAT'S THE HARM?

1. See, e.g., "A Vermont Court Speaks," editorial, *Boston Globe*, December 22, 1999: "[Gay marriage] no more undermine[s] traditional marriage than sailing undermines swimming."

2. But for evidence, see Mary Douglas, *How Institutions Think* (New York: Syracuse University Press, 1986). See also Robert P. George, *Making Men Moral: Civil Liberties and Public Morality* (Oxford: Clarendon Press, 1993).

3. Joseph Raz, "Autonomy and Pluralism," in *The Morality of Freedom* (Oxford: Clarendon Press, 1988): 393.

4. Patrick Lee, Robert P. George, and Gerard V. Bradley, "Marriage and Procreation: Avoiding Bad Arguments," *Public Discourse*, March 30, 2011, http://www.thepublicdiscourse.com/2011/03/2637.

5. See also Andrew Cherlin, *The Marriage-Go-Round* (New York: Knopf, 2009), for a discussion of the link between the rise of expressive individualism and the divorce revolution.

6. For recent research showing that an expressive model of relationships is associated with an increased risk of divorce, see W. Bradford Wilcox and Jeffrey Dew, "Is Love a Flimsy Foundation? Soulmate versus Institutional Models of Marriage," *Social Science Research* 39 (2010): 687, http://www.sciencedirect .com/science?ob=ArticleURL&_udi=B6WX8-506W6K9-1&_ user=709071&_coverDate. For research showing that same-sex unions tend more often to eschew sexual exclusivity, see Scott James, "Many Successful Gay Marriages Share an Open Secret," *New York Times*, January 28, 2010, http://www.nytimes .com/2010/01/29/us/29sfmetro.html?ref=us.

7. Temporary marriage licenses have recently been considered in Mexico City: see Christina Ng, "Mexico City Considers Temporary Marriage Licenses," September 30, 2011, http://abcnews.go .com/blogs/headlines/2011/09/mexico-city-considers-temporary -marriage-licenses/.

8. Richard Doerflinger, "Family Policy in the United States" (1980), http://www.usccb.org/prolife/tdocs/FaithfulForLife.pdf. Maggie Gallagher, *The Abolition of Marriage: How We Destroy Lasting Love* (Washington, D.C.: Regnery Publishing, 1996). *Promises to Keep: Decline and Renewal of Marriage in America*, edited by David Popenoe, Jean Bethke Elshtain, and David Blankenhorn (Lanham, Md.: Rowman and Littlefield Publishers, 1996). *The Book of Marriage: The Wisest Answers to the Toughest Questions*, edited by Dana Mack and David Blankenhorn (Grand Rapids, Mich.: Eerdmans Publishing, 2001). *The Fatherhood Movement: A Call to Action*, edited by Wade F. Horn, David Blankenhorn, and Mitchell B. Pearlstein (Lanham, Md.: Lexington Books, 1999). United States Conference of Catholic Bishops, "Marriage and Family Life" (1975), http://www.usccb.org/prolife/programs/ rlp/Marriage&FamilyLife75.pdf. Maggie Gallagher and Barbara Dafoe Whitehead, "End No-Fault Divorce?" *First Things* 75 (1997): 24.

9. Sara McLanahan and Gary Sandefur, *Growing Up with a Single Parent: What Hurts, What Helps* (Cambridge, Mass.: Harvard University Press, 1994). Bruce J. Ellis, John E. Bates, Kenneth A.

Dodge, et al., "Does Father Absence Place Daughters at Special Risk for Early Sexual Activity and Teenage Pregnancy?" *Child Development* 74 (2003): 801–21. Wilcox, Doherty, Fisher, et al., *Why Marriage Matters* (cited in chap. 3, n. 11). Lorraine Blackman, Obie Clayton, Norval Glenn, et al., *The Consequences of Marriage for African Americans: A Comprehensive Literature Review* (New York: Institute for American Values, 2005).

10. Elizabeth Marquardt, *Family Structure and Children's Educational Outcomes* (New York: Institute for American Values, 2005). Paul R. Amato, "The Impact of Family Formation Change on the Cognitive, Social, and Emotional Well-Being of the Next Generation," *The Future of Children* 15 (2005): 75–96. Cynthia Harper and Sara McLanahan, "Father Absence and Youth Incarceration," *Journal of Research on Adolescence* 14 (2004): 369–97.

11. David Popenoe, *Life without Father: Compelling New Evidence That Fatherhood and Marriage Are Indispensable for the Good of Children and Society* (New York: Free Press, 1996), 146.

12. Ibid., 197.

13. W. Bradford Wilcox, "Reconcilable Differences: What Social Sciences Show about the Complementarity of the Sexes and Parenting," *Touchstone* 18, no. 9 (November 2005): 36.

14. Michael J. Rosenfeld, "Nontraditional Families and Childhood Progress through School," *Demography* 47 (2010): 755–75, http://www.stanford.edu/~mrosenfe/Rosenfeld_Nontraditional_ Families_Demography.pdf.

15. See, e.g., Charlotte J. Patterson, "Children of Lesbian and Gay Parents," in *Advances in Clinical Child Psychology*, vol. 19, edited by Thomas H. Ollendick and Ronald J. Prinz, 235–82 (New York: Plenum, 1997). Fiona Tasker, "Lesbian Mothers, Gay Fathers, and Their Children: A Review," *Developmental and Behavioral Pediatrics* 26, no. 3 (2005): 224–40.

16. For studies that use snowball sampling, see, e.g., Henny M. W. Bos, Frank van Balen, and Dymphna C. van den Boom, "Child Adjustment and Parenting in Planned Lesbian Parent Families," *American Journal of Orthopsychiatry* 77 (2007): 38–48. Anne Brewaeys, Ingrid Ponjaert, Eylard V. Van Hall, and Susan Golombok, "Donor Insemination: Child Development and Family Functioning in Lesbian Mother Families," *Human Reproduction* 12 (1997): 1349–59. Megan Fulcher, Erin L. Sutfin, and Charlotte J. Patterson, "Individual Differences in Gender Development: Associations with Parental Sexual Orientation, Attitudes, and Division of Labor," *Sex*

Roles 57 (2008): 330–41. Theodora Sirota, "Adult Attachment Style Dimensions in Women Who Have Gay or Bisexual Fathers," *Archives of Psychiatric Nursing* 23, no. 4 (2009): 289–97. Katrien Vanfraussen, Ingrid Ponjaert-Kristoffersen, and Anne Brewaeys, "Family Functioning in Lesbian Families Created by Donor Insemination," *American Journal of Orthopsychiatry* 73, no. 1 (2003): 78–90.

17. Sven Berg, "Snowball Sampling," in *Encyclopedia of Statistical Sciences,* vol. 8, edited by Samuel Kotz and Norman L. Johnson, 528–32 (New York: Wiley-Interscience, 1988).

18. Abbie E. Goldberg, *Lesbian and Gay Parents and Their Children: Research on the Family Life Cycle* (Washington, D.C.: APA Books, 2010), 12–13.

19. See, e.g., Nanette K. Gartrell, Henny M. W. Bos, and Naomi G. Goldberg, "Adolescents of the U.S. National Longitudinal Lesbian Family Study: Sexual Orientation, Sexual Behavior, and Sexual Risk Exposure," *Archives of Sexual Behavior* 40 (2011): 1199–1209.

20. Loren Marks, "Same-sex Parenting and Children's Outcomes: A Closer Examination of the American Psychological Association's Brief on Lesbian and Gay Parenting," *Social Science Research* 41 (2012): 735–51, 748, http://ac.els-cdn.com/S0049089X12000580/1-s2.0-S0049089X12000580-main.pdf?_tid=8b0a9f5c-04d1-11e2-9a3e-00000aacb35f&acdnat=1348331060_c1ca19d8556b56fd70caafb54ea54c69.

21. Mark Regnerus, "How Different Are the Adult Children of Parents Who Have Same-Sex Relationships? Findings from the New Family Structures Study," *Social Science Research* 41 (2012): 752–70.

22. Paul Amato, "The Well-Being of Children with Gay and Lesbian Parents," *Social Science Research* 41 (2012): 771–74.

23. Timothy J. Biblarz and Judith Stacey, "How Does the Gender of Parents Matter?" *Journal of Marriage and Family* 72 (2010): 3. For other criticisms of the samples on which available studies have been based, see Steven L. Nock, "Affidavit of Steven Nock," *Halpern et al. v. Canada and MCCT v. Canada.* ON S.C.D.C. (2001), http://marriagelaw.cua.edu/Law/cases/Canada/ontario/halpern/aff_nock.pdf. Ellen C. Perrin, "Technical Report: Coparent or Second-Parent Adoption by Same-Sex Partners," *Pediatrics* 109 (2002): 341–44. Richard R. Redding, "It's Really about Sex: Same-Sex Marriage, Lesbigay Parenting, and the Psychology of Disgust," *Duke Journal of Gender Law and Policy* 16 (2008): 127–93.

24. William Meezan and Jonathan Rauch, "Gay Marriage, Same-Sex Parenting, and America's Children," *Future of Children* 15 (2005): 97–115.

25. Susan L. Brown, "Family Structure and Child Well-Being: The Significance of Parental Cohabitation," *Journal of Marriage and Family* 66, no. 2 (2004): 351–67. Wendy D. Manning, Pamela J. Smock, and Debarun Majumdar, "The Relative Stability of Cohabiting and Marital Unions for Children," *Population Research and Policy Review* 23 (2004): 135–59. McLanahan and Sandefur, *Growing Up with a Single Parent* (cited above, n. 9).

26. McLanahan and Sandefur, *Growing Up with a Single Parent* (cited above, n. 9), 1.

27. For example, the Internal Revenue Service revoked the tax-exempt status of Bob Jones University because of its racially discriminatory practices, and the Supreme Court upheld this action as compatible with the university's First Amendment rights.

28. "TV Host Fired over Sean Avery Debate," *ESPN.com*, May 13, 2011, at http://sports.espn.go.com/new-york/nhl/news/story?id= 6532954.

29. *Walden v. Centers for Disease Control*, Case No. 1:08-cv-02278 -JEC, U.S. District Court, Northern District of Georgia, March 18, 2010, http://www.telladf.org/UserDocs/WaldenSJorder.pdf.

30. Jill P. Capuzzo, "Group Loses Tax Break over Gay Union Issue," *New York Times*, September 18, 2007, http://www.nytimes .com/2007/09/18/nyregion/18grove.html?_r=0.

31. George F. Will, "The Tangled Web of Conflicting Rights," *Washington Post*, September 14, 2012, http://www.washingtonpost .com/opinions/george-f-will-the-tangled-web-of-conflicting -rights/2012/09/14/95b787c2-fddc-11e1-b153-218509a954e1_ story.html.

32. Marc D. Stern, "Same-Sex Marriage and the Churches," in *Same-Sex Marriage and Religious Liberty: Emerging Conflicts*, edited by Douglas Laycock, Anthony Picarello, and Robin Fretwell Wilson, 1–57 (Lanham, Md.: Rowman and Littlefield, 2008), 1, 11–14. This collection of essays includes the views of scholars on both sides of the same-sex marriage question, who conclude that conflicts with religious liberty are inevitable when marriage is extended to same-sex couples.

33. Maggie Gallagher, "Banned in Boston: The Coming Conflict between Same-Sex Marriage and Religious Liberty," *The Weekly*

Standard, May 5, 2006, http://www.weeklystandard.com/Content/Public/Articles/000/000/012/191kgwgh.asp.

34. See, e.g., *Parker v. Hurley*, 514 F.3d 87 (1st Cir. 2008).

35. Becket Fund for Religious Liberty, *Same-Sex Marriage and State Anti-Discrimination Laws* (Washington, D.C.: Becket Fund for Religious Liberty, January 2009), 2, http://www.becketfund.org/wp-content/uploads/2011/04/Same-Sex-Marriage-and-State-Anti-Discrimination-Laws-with-Appendices.pdf.

36. Monica Hesse, "Opposing Gay Unions with Sanity and a Smile," *Washington Post*, August 28, 2009.

37. Andrew Alexander, " 'Sanity and a Smile' and an Outpouring of Rage," *Washington Post*, September 6, 2009.

38. Frank Rich, "The Bigots' Last Hurrah," Op-Ed Columnist, *New York Times*, April 19, 2009.

39. See, e.g., Human Rights Campaign, http://www.hrc.org (self-identifying the organization as a 501(c)(4) advocacy group "working for lesbian, gay, bisexual, and transgender equal rights"); Annie Stockwell, "Stop the Hate: Vote No on 8," Advocate.com, August 20, 2008, http://www.advocate.com/Arts_and_Entertainment/People/Stop_the_Hate (framing opposition to California's Proposition 8, which provides that "only marriage between a man and a woman is valid or recognized in California," as a struggle against hate).

40. *Perry v. Brown*, 671 F.3d 1052, February 7, 2011, 36.

41. For more on the effects of a sexualized culture on friendship, see Anthony Esolen, "A Requiem for Friendship: Why Boys Will Not Be Boys and Other Consequences of the Sexual Revolution," *Touchstone* 18 (September 2005): 21, http://www.touchstonemag.com/archives/article.php?id=18-07-021-f.

42. 2 Samuel 1:26; Augustine, *Confessions* 4.75–77.

43. Traditional marriage laws, by contrast, merely encourage adherence to norms in relationships where those norms already have a rational basis. See chapter 2 on comprehensive commitment.

44. See Gallagher, "(How) Will Gay Marriage Weaken Marriage as a Social Institution" (cited in chap. 1, n. 3), 62.

45. "Beyond Same-Sex Marriage" (cited in chap. 1, n. 7).

46. Brake, "Minimal Marriage" (cited in chap. 1, n. 12), 336, 323.

47. Andrew Sullivan, "Introduction," in *Same-Sex Marriage: Pro and Con: A Reader*, edited by Andrew Sullivan, 1st ed. (New York: Vintage Books, 1997), xvii, xix.

48. E. J. Graff, "Retying the Knot," in ibid., 134, 136.

49. Ibid., 137.

50. Andrew Sullivan, *Virtually Normal: An Argument about Homosexuality* (New York: Vintage Books, 1996), 202–3.

51. Ari Karpel, "Monogamish," *The Advocate*, July 7, 2011, http://www.advocate.com/Print_Issue/Features/Monogamish/.

52. See http://www.advocate.com/arts-entertainment/features?page=7.

53. Victoria A. Brownworth, "Something Borrowed, Something Blue: Is Marriage Right for Queers?" in *I Do/I Don't: Queers on Marriage*, edited by Greg Wharton and Ian Philips (San Francisco: Suspect Thoughts Press, 2004), 53, 58–59.

54. Ellen Willis, "Can Marriage Be Saved? A Forum," *The Nation*, July 5, 2004, 16.

55. Michelangelo Signorile, "Bridal Wave," *Out* 42 (December–January 1994): 68, 161.

56. Ibid.

57. "Mexico City Proposes Temporary Marriage Licenses" (cited in chap. 1, n. 10).

58. Julia Zebley, "Utah Polygamy Law Challenged in Federal Lawsuit," *Jurist*, July 13, 2011, http://jurist.org/paperchase/2011/07/utah-polygamy-law-challenged-in-federal-lawsuit.php.

59. "Three-Person Civil Union Sparks Controversy in Brazil" (cited in chap. 1, n. 9).

60. See generally Jonathan Rauch, *Gay Marriage: Why It Is Good for Gays, Good for Straights, and Good for America* (New York: Henry Holt & Co., 2005).

61. David P. McWhirter and Andrew M. Mattison, *The Male Couple: How Relationships Develop* (Englewood Cliffs, N.J.: Prentice-Hall Trade, 1984), 252–53.

62. Ibid., 3.

63. James, "Many Successful Gay Marriages Share an Open Secret" (cited above, n. 6).

64. Ibid.

65. Trevor A. Hart and Danielle R. Schwartz, "Cognitive-Behavioral Erectile Dysfunction Treatment for Gay Men," *Cognitive and Behavior Practice* 17 (February 2010): 66.

66. Alfred DeMaris, "Distal and Proximal Influences on the Risk of Extramarital Sex: A Prospective Study of Longer Duration Marriages," *Journal of Sex Research* 46 (2009): 597.

67. Julie H. Hall and Frank D. Fincham, "Psychological Distress: Precursor or Consequence of Dating Infidelity," *Personality and So-*

cial Psychology Bulletin 35 (2009): 143, http://psp.sagepub.com/content/35/2/143.short.

68. Popenoe, *Life without Father* (cited above, n. 11). Mark Regnerus and Jeremy Uecker, *Premarital Sex in America* (New York: Oxford University Press, 2011).

69. C. H. Mercer, G. J. Hart, A. M. Johnson, and J. A. Cassell, "Behaviourally Bisexual Men as a Bridge Population for HIV and Sexually Transmitted Infections? Evidence from a National Probability Survey," *International Journal of STD and AIDS* 20 (2009): 87, 88.

70. Edward O. Laumann, J. H. Gagnon, R. T. Michael, and S. Michaels, *The Social Organization of Sexuality: Sexual Practices in the United States* (Chicago: University of Chicago Press, 1994), 314–16.

71. Ibid.

72. James, "Many Successful Gay Marriages Share an Open Secret" (cited above, n. 6).

CHAPTER 5: JUSTICE AND EQUALITY

1. Macedo, "Homosexuality and the Conservative Mind" (cited in Introduction, n. 3), 261, 279. Andrew Koppelman, *The Gay Rights Question in Contemporary American Law* (Chicago: University of Chicago Press, 2002), 87–88.

2. Andrew Koppelman has argued that "[a] sterile person's genitals are no more suitable for generation than an unloaded gun is suitable for shooting. If someone points a gun at me and pulls the trigger, he exhibits the behavior which, as behavior, is suitable for shooting, but it still matters a lot whether the gun is loaded and whether he knows it"; Koppelman, ibid.

   Koppelman's objection is mistaken and misses an important point. We can properly say that man-made objects and artificial processes are ordered or directed toward certain goals only so long as we use them for those goals. This in turn presupposes that we think them capable of actually realizing those goals. That is, the function of man-made objects and processes is imposed on them by the human beings who use them. Thus, a piece of metal becomes a knife—an artifact whose function is to cut—only when we intend to use it for cutting. When it is no longer capable of cutting and we no longer intend to use it for cutting, it is no longer really a knife.

   The same does not hold for the union between a man and a woman's bodies, however, because natural organs are what they are independently of what we intend to use them for and even of whether the function they characteristically serve can be brought to completion. Thus, in our example, a stomach remains a stomach—an organ whose natural function is to play a certain role in digestion—regardless of whether we intend it to be used that way and even of whether digestion will be successfully completed. Something analogous is true of sexual organs with respect to reproduction.

3. See, e.g., Eskridge, Jr., "A History of Same-Sex Marriage" (cited in chap. 3, n. 29), 1419, 1424.

4. See, e.g., ibid.

5. Ibid.

6. See *Loving v. Virginia*, 388 U.S. 1, 11 (1967).

CHAPTER 6: A CRUEL BARGAIN?

1. See Introduction, n. 4.

2. See Ryan Conrad, ed., *Against Equality: Queer Critiques of Gay Marriage* (New York: Against Equality Press, 2010). See also Doug Mainwaring, "Why I Oppose Gay Marriage," Opinions, *Washington Post*, September 21, 2012, http://www.washingtonpost.com/opinions/why-i-oppose-gay-marriage/2012/09/21/1cd0056c-02a2-11e2-91e7-2962c74e7738_story.html?socialreader_check=0&denied=1.

3. John Heard, "Relationship Registers: What Does Justice Demand?" *Dreadnought*, March 11, 2008, http://johnheard.blogspot.com/2008/03/dreadtalk-relationship-registers-what.html.

4. Andrew Sullivan, "Only the Right Kind of Symbolic Sex," *The Daily Dish*, August 4, 2009, http://andrewsullivan.theatlantic.com/the_daily_dish/2009/08/only-the-right-kind-of-symbolic-sex.html.

5. See, e.g., Katherine M. Franke, "Same-Sex Marriage Is a Mixed Blessing," *New York Times*, June 23, 2011, http://www.nytimes.com/2011/06/24/opinion/24franke.html.

6. Ryan T. Anderson and Sherif Girgis, "A Real Compromise on the Same-Sex Marriage Debate: An Invitation to Rauch and Blankenhorn," *Public Discourse*, February 24, 2009, http://www.thepublicdiscourse.com/2009/02/84/.

7. Blankenhorn, *The Future of Marriage* (cited in chap. 3, n. 2), xix. See also Jonathan Rauch, "The Equal Dignity of Homosexual Love," *Independent Gay Forum*, September 12, 2007, http://igfculturewatch.com/2007/09/12/the-equal-dignity-of-homosexual-love/.

APPENDIX: FURTHER REFLECTIONS ON BODILY UNION

1. Parts of this section originally appeared in Sherif Girgis, Robert P. George, and Ryan T. Anderson, "Marriage: Real Bodily Union," *Public Discourse*, December 30, 2010, http://www.thepublic discourse.com/2010/12/2277/.

2. Barry Deutsch, "What Is Bodily Union? (A Response to 'What Is Marriage?')," *FamilyScholars*, December 21, 2010, http://family scholars.org/2010/12/21/what-is-bodily-union-a-response-to-what -is-marriage/. All subsequent quotations of Deutsch are from this essay.

3. Sherif Girgis, Robert P. George, and Ryan T. Anderson, "What Is Marriage?" *Harvard Journal of Law and Public Policy* 34 (2010): 243–87, 254.

4. Ibid., 255.

5. We have raised many challenges to the revisionist view of marriage. As a challenge to our own, some ask about permanently unconsummated unions—say, a paraplegic man's. Could these count as comprehensive unions, and thus marriages?

   According to the conjugal view, a marriage is certainly *incomplete* without consummation. And in a strong version of this view, perhaps even forming marital *consent* requires intending (and thus expecting) to consummate. In that case, marital consent involves at least a conditional promise to consummate—say, upon a reasonable request. (In this connection, Catholic readers will find it interesting that Thomas Aquinas, who believed Joseph and Mary to be married despite the latter's perpetual virginity, inferred that they must have consented to consummating, but on a condition—i.e., if God so willed—that they never thought was fulfilled.)

   In this version of the conjugal view, the paraplegic's relationship is not even an incomplete marriage. Still, a good marriage policy would go on recognizing it. For inquiring into its true status would be invasive (in *what* is asked, not just *how*), and recognizing it would not negate the *public* understanding of marriage as a conjugal union.

   In a softer version of the conjugal view, perhaps, a couple *could* make the correct commitment for a marriage—they could marry— so long as they could *in principle* consummate their commitment (assuming that it is also lifelong, etc.). Maybe the paraplegic's relationship is just on a spectrum with other opposite-sex unions: each *could* consummate given normal conditions, such as good health and time to reach arousal.

Each version finds some support among traditional-marriage advocates. Whichever is more plausible overall, the strong version has counterintuitive implications for some people on *this* question. But even with them, we submit, the conjugal view would trump the revisionist.

On *any* moral issue, a fully consistent account will likely contradict the prevailing public view somewhere, for "the" prevailing view is just an aggregate of many people's mostly pre-theoretic intuitions, shaped by many factors, only some of which are reliable. It is where we start our reasoning, but rarely where we end. Yet the conjugal view remains the coherent line of the *best* fit with our practices, experience, and judgments about how human beings are constituted (as mind-body unities) and how distinct goods like friendship are structured. After all, the revisionist view has no basis in principle—none—for distinguishing marriage from companionship.

6. Jason Lee Steorts, "Two Views of Marriage, and the Falsity of the Choice between Them," *National Review*, April 4, 2011, http://www.nationalreview.com/articles/263672/two-views-marriage-and-falsity-choice-between-them-jason-lee-steorts.

Index